How to Fix American V-Twin Motorcycles

Shadley Bros.

Published by:
Wolfgang Publications Inc.
Stillwater, MN 55082
www.wolfpub.com

Legals

First published in 2009 by Wolfgang Publications Inc., PO Box 223, Stillwater MN 55082

© Shadley Bros., 2009, 2012

All rights reserved. With the exception of quoting brief passages for the purposes of review no part of this publication may be reproduced without prior written permission from the publisher.

The information in this book is true and complete to the best of our knowledge. All recommendations are made without any guarantee on the part of the author or publisher, who also disclaim any liability incurred in connection with the use of this data or specific details.

We recognize that some words, model names and designations, for example, mentioned herein are the property of the trademark holder. We use them for identification purposes only. This is not an official publication.

ISBN: 1-929133-72-3
ISBN 13: 978-1-929133-72-7

Printed and bound in USA.

How to Fix American V-Twin Motorcycles

Chapter One
      The Shadley Brothers 6

Chapter Two
      Oil Change 10

Chapter Three
      Brakes 16

Chapter Four
      The Primary Drive 36

Chapter Five
      Electrical 48

Chapter Six
      Tires, Wheels, Bearings 68

Chapter Seven
      Forks & Neck 88

Chapter Eight
      Shocks 106

Chapter Nine
      Tune-Up 114

Chapter Ten
      Storage 132

Chapter Eleven
      Dyno 138

Catalog & Sources 142

Acknowledgements

We would like to thank the following people for all their help and for their influence in the way we look at things.

J.P. Shadley, our Dad, who always showed us how NOT to do things.

Tom Tighe, my first and only boss, the man who employed me (Mark Shadley) from age 13 to 26, when we opened our first real garage.

Dave Perewitz, for introducing us to the custom motorcycle world in the mid-1970s. We had bikes before we met David, but after that we really became custom bike people.

Tim Remus, for his friendship over the years and his help putting this book together.

From the Publisher

I first met Mark and Paul Shadley someplace in the early 1990s. As happens so often in the motorcycle community, it all started in Sturgis. First there were the photo shoots of Shadley bikes I did for American Iron magazine. What impressed me about a Shadley-built bike was the nice paint, the correct proportions and the way everything fit. It wasn't until a few years later that I started to ride with Mark and Paul. Some people say custom bikes never get ridden - really ridden. Those folks have never experienced a ride with the Shadleys. Anyone who can build a bike from scratch that not only looks awesome, but also runs like the proverbial bat out of hell, has to be a great mechanic. Which is why Mark and Paul Shadley are the ideal authors for this book about how to keep your motorcycle in perfect mechanical health.

Timothy Remus

Introduction

There are at least two good reasons to do your own maintenance and basic repairs to that V-Twin in the garage.

First, there's the pride of doing it yourself. After you've finished with even a simple job, there's that feeling of accomplishment that's hard find in any other way.

Second, you've saved money. Whether it's an oil change or a new set of brake pads, you save twice; by performing your own work and buying the parts at less than retail prices.

We've tried to provide how-to information and abundant photos on all the basic maintenance and repair chores you're likely to encounter. If you've never done an oil change, we have you covered in the first chapter. The rest of the book walks you through brake service, how to remove and install a front or rear tire, and how to replace the tire on the rim.

Servicing the primary drive and clutch is the most difficult job we cover here. Even if you decide this particular task is over your head, at least you will understand what's involved before asking someone else to do the job.

Some of what we've covered is simply too specialized for anyone at home to perform, like a dyno test. We dedicated one chapter to the process simply so you understand what's involved in this increasingly common procedure, and what you should get for your money.

And though we've included specific procedures and specifications for most of the jobs documented in this book, we don't provide torque specifications for all models of all Harley-Davidsons or aftermarket bikes. Which is why we recommend that you buy a factory service manual for your bike. That way you have all the capacities and all the specifications for your particular model.

Don't be embarrassed at what you don't know, or the fact that you never did an oil change or a brake job before. Everyone starts somewhere. Whether you're thirteen or thirty-three, the important thing is the learning and the fact that in most cases you *can* do it yourself.

Chapter One

The Shadley Bros.

Born to the Garage

THE BEGINNINGS – MARK SHADLEY

You might say I was born to be a mechanic, because I started helping out at a garage when I was thirteen years old. That turned into a full time job, and I worked there for another thirteen years. The guy I worked for was a really good mechanic and I learned a lot from him. During part of that time I also went to trade school.

Eventually I decided to work for myself. With no shop or even a garage to work in, all

Along with all the other motorcycle work, we build almost a dozen custom bikes each year. We built this one for Paul (sitting on the bike) and he calls it his tail-dragger.

Dino Petrocelli

the work had to be done in the driveway at home. By that time my brother Paul had been working in a gas station for a number of years. So after working our regular jobs we would meet at my house and work in the driveway almost every night. We did that for a year and a half, in all kinds of weather.

In 1981 I started AutoTec with my brother Paul. That's when we rented a building and took out our first business license. At first I kept my regular job and worked there at night. After six or eight months I quit the other job and went to work full time for myself.

Motorcycles are a Constant

I was building bikes before I started my first job. In high school I always owned a bike or two, and at least one was under construction at any time. Customizing bikes turned into a secondary hobby. Eventually it grew to the point where I was always building a bike on the side, and working on other people's bikes too.

When we moved AutoTec, out auto repair business, into the new building eight years ago, I decided to open a true motorcycle store and repair facility. I didn't want the motorcycles to be a hobby or part time

I built this rubber-mount bike in the mid-1990s, based on an Arlen Ness rubber-mount frame with my own swingarm and inboard rear brake. This is the back side of Devil's Tower in Wyoming, Paul and I've been riding these roads for years and years.

We built this bike in the late 1990s, using one of the Arlen Ness Luxury Liner packages. Instead of running a motor with a lot of cubic inches, I added a turbo kit to an 80 inch Evo.

deal anymore. I wanted Shadley Bros to be an integral part of the overall business.

When we designed the new building I left one, some-what small, room for the motorcycle shop, and a bigger room on the same end of the building for the motorcycle parts store. Right away though, we outgrew the motorcycle shop and had to move it to a much bigger room on the other end of the building. Now we've added a dyno facility in that same corner of the building. That was a big deal, not only because the dyno is expensive, but because to do it right you have to build a whole separate room.

Current Work Load

We've built up the Shadley Bros. business over a period of time, it definitely did not happen overnight. The business has grown from being a hobby to being a full time business, an essential part of our overall operation.

In the winter we have one full time mechanic and one full time fabricator, and Paul and I help of course. We store over 50 bikes in the winter. It's a good deal for the customers because the bikes are stored correctly in a controlled environment, and it's a good deal for us because we do service on most of the bikes we store. We step it up when the season really hits. In the spring and summer there are three to four full time employees working in the motorcycle store and the motorcycle repair shop.

We do a lot of basic service and maintenance, along with engine hop ups, and collision work. We have an in-house paint facility so the collision work is a natural for us. That small space

My brother Paul in Spearfish, South Dakota (just west of Sturgis) with one of his FXRs.

Here I'm working on the final assembly of a K-model that we built recently. I like all the bikes, from new Twin Cams to the old Sportsters and Panheads.

that I originally set aside to be the motorcycle shop has turned into the assembly shop for the custom bikes we build. Every year we build eight to ten custom bikes. And we also build a few raffle bikes for the local police and fire departments.

Whether it's fabricating of parts for a custom bike, or doing a valve job on a Harley, we try to do everything in-house. We do the fabrication and the finish work here. We have a frame jig, a tubing bender, and a machine shop so we can build almost anything. The only work we don't do here is chrome plating and polishing.

The most exciting thing we've done lately is add the dyno. It makes trouble shooting so much easier, and it's a great tool not just for getting the most power from a bike, but for breaking in new bikes and checking their operation without having to do a series of long road tests.

Shadley Bros. is a nice addition, a compliment, to our other business. It's grown a lot just since we've moved into the new building. Even when the economy is slow, we still have plenty of work. We have a good crew and a good reputation. When I look down the road I just see more bikes and more growth.

We've built a number of side-hacks, the difference in this one is we decided to keep it for ourselves. The drivetrain came from a late-model Sportster. The bike isn't real fast, but it's a absolute ball to ride.

For a small store we stock a lot of parts, and anything we don't have is available in only one or two days.

Chapter Two
Oil Change
Essential Maintenance

The oil and filter change you do on a regular basis is the most important regular maintenance you do for that motorcycle. You also need to make sure the oil is at the right level. Make sure you check the oil every couple of tanks, because even a new bike can develop an oil leak.

How it Works

The oil performs three major tasks: it lubricates, cools, and cleans the engine. Everyone knows that the oil prevents metal-to-metal contact in the engine. Oil also helps to cool the engine. Twin Cam engines have oil jets that squirt oil up

Here's a Harley Davidson Twin Cam Softail in for minor service. When your bike needs service depends on mileage, time and how you use the bike.

against the bottom of the piston to help remove the heat of combustion. An engine that's low on oil will run hotter. Oil cleans the motor by keeping dirt in suspension so it can be picked up by the filter.

There are two types of oil, mineral based and synthetic. There is nothing wrong with mineral based oil, and for break-in of a new engine we recommend mineral-based oil in the viscosity recommended by the manufacturer. Once the motor is broken in though, we think synthetic oil is a good upgrade.

We like synthetic oil because it stands up better to heat. When the motor gets good and hot, mineral oil tends to burn, or carbonize, and turn to a varnish. It looses the lubrication quality. Synthetic oil can run considerably hotter before this happens. No matter what type you normally run, if you're a long way from home and run low on oil, any oil is better than none, or not enough oil.

How Often

We like to see a new engine get its first oil change at 250 miles. Harley says 1000 miles, but we think oil is cheap. The first few hundred miles is when the engine is breaking in, all those metal parts are getting to know each other and shearing off little pieces of metal. You want to get all those contaminants out of there as quickly as possible. After that we recommend oil changes every 2,500 miles, more often if the bike has been ridden really hard or if you've been stuck in traffic.

Before you change the oil, take the bike for a ride so the oil is warm and the dirt is held in suspension, and not sitting on the bottom of the crankcase or oil tank. Don't overfill the oil tank. If you do, you can plug the oil case vent, which may pop out some seals

Oil Filters

Not all filters are the same. The filter media is rated in microns, or how small a particle will be filtered out. The important thing is to buy a brand name filter, and to remember that the Evo and Twin Cam use a different filter.

Dispose of the used oil properly, most places that sell oil will take your oil back. Don't just dump it in the garbage of the back yard. And don't contaminate it with water as that messes up the recycling effort.

Always warm the motor prior to draining oil. When warm, the oil flows better, and any dirt is more likely to be held in suspension by the oil.

Remove the filler cap when draining the oil to allow a better flow. Make sure the oil tank is warm to the touch.

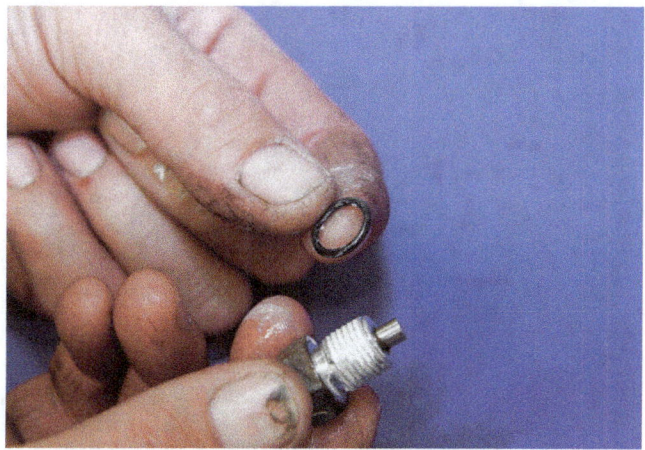

We like to put liquid thread sealer and a new O-ring on the oil plug.

1. After all of the oil is drained out you can use either an Allen wrench or socket wrench to re-install the oil plug.

4. Put a thin film of oil on the new filter before installing it on the engine.

2. Typical oil filter and oil filter oil drain funnels. Note, Twin Cam and Evo filters are not the same.

5. Clean the oil filter contact area and be sure the old oil filter seal is removed - occasionally they stick to the oil filter boss.

3. Fill oil filter prior to installing it on Twin Cam motors. Always change the filter when you change the oil.

6. Install the filter, hand tighten only. Don't over tighten it with a wrench.

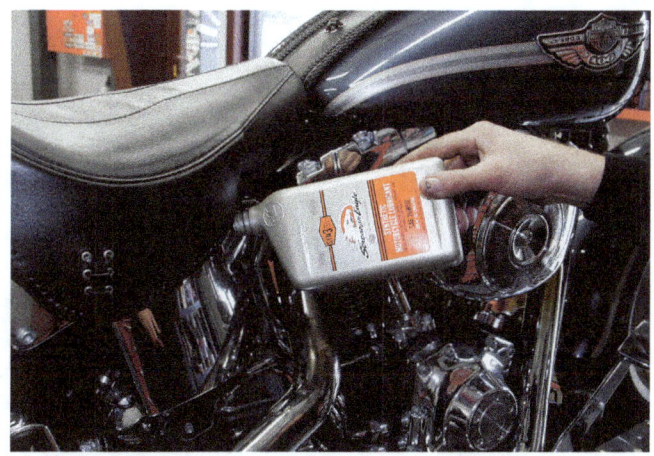

1. Refill oil. Run the engine and check the level while warm. We like the HD Synthetic 3 oil. It can be used in the motor, transmission and primary drive.

4. Unscrew the transmission filler/dipstick plug. Check the level and make sure it looks clean on the middle to upper level of the stick.

2. Not all oils are the same, modern motors use multi-weight synthetic or petroleum base. Older models use heavier weights. If in doubt check the manual or ask at the shop.

5. Always check the tire pressure. After a period of non-usage some tires will go low on pressure.

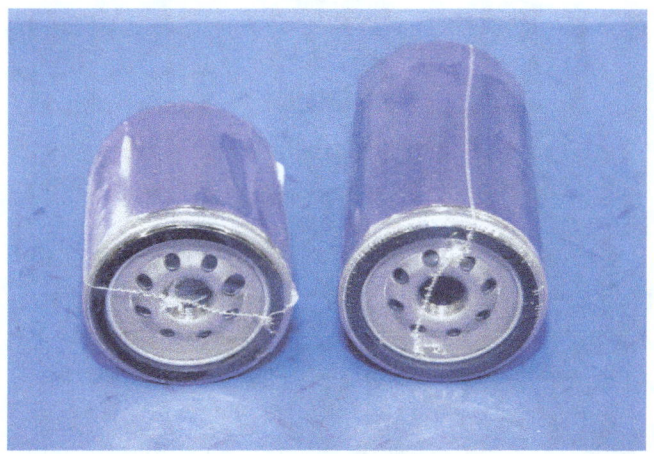

3. Not all filters are the same. Twin Cam and Evos take a different filter, be sure to use the right one.

6. Visually check and inspect the brake pads for worn lining. If they get too worn they will score the brake rotors.

Tool Time

You don't have to buy a ten thousand dollar set of Snap-On tools just to do routine maintenance on your Bagger or Softail. All you really need is a basic set of tools from a company like Sears. The set should include quarter inch, and three-eighths inch socket sets, along with a good set of combination wrenches. Additional necessary tools include screwdrivers, a set of pliers, a wire cutter, maybe a channel lock wrench, and some vise grips. With any luck you already have a tire gauge and use it on a regular basis to monitor the pressure in the tires.

That basic set will include most, but not all, of the tools you need to work on a late-model Harley-Davidson or aftermarket bike. The other items you need include a good set of Allen wrenches, a set of Torx drivers and an oil filter wrench. To ensure all your fasteners are tightened correctly, you will need at least one, probably two, torque wrenches, one to measure foot pounds and another to measure inch pounds.

A digital multi-meter is a very handy thing to have as well, and once you have a meter you're likely to wonder how you ever lived all those years without one.

Though not exactly tools, it's handy to have a range of lubricants on hand. WD-40 is a great multipurpose light lube. Good for everything from freeing up rusty bolts to lubricating throttle and clutch cables. Some white lithium-type lube is handy when you want something heavier than WD-40, and wheel bearing grease can be used anytime a heavy and durable lubricant is required. And if you're fixing Harleys, you just have to have some anti-seize.

The other thing you don't need is a thousand dollar drive-on Handy-Lift. For about a hundred bucks you can get a parallelogram-style lift that slides under the frame and lifts the bike up off the floor far enough to change tires and do basic service.

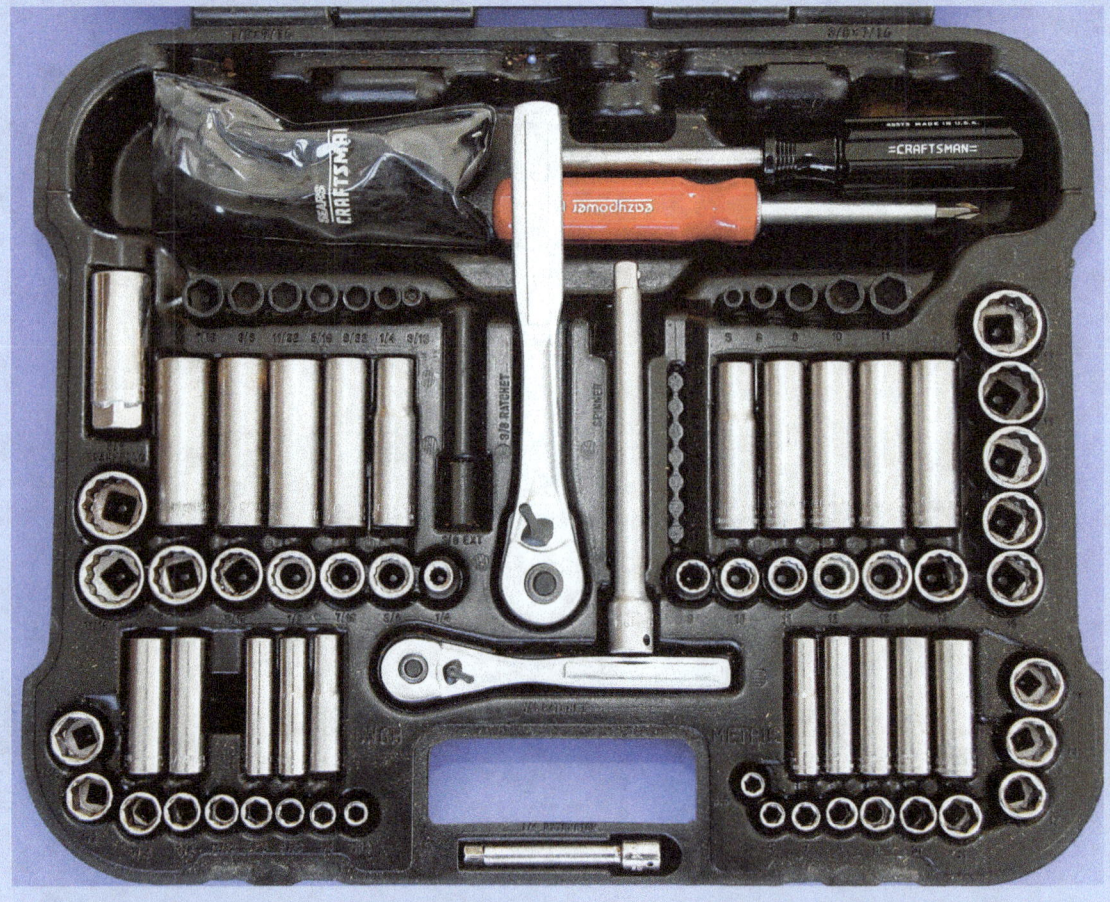

Everybody wants the big tool set with the mega lower box. You can get started though with just a small set of tools, and then just add as your needs and budget grow.

Tool Time

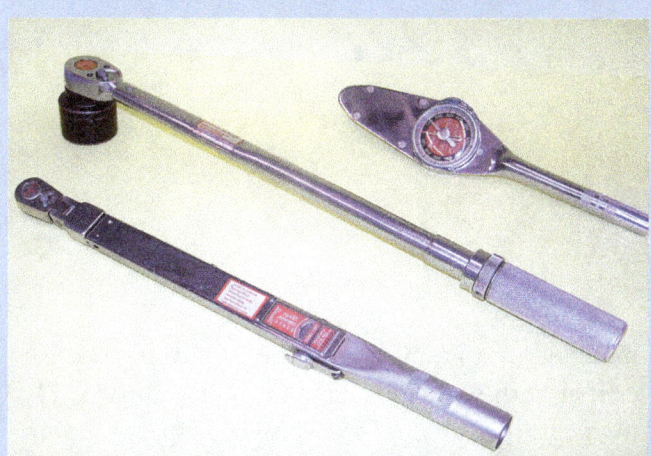

Torque wrenches come in various designs and ranges.

These are some of the lubricants that we keep on hand in our shop.

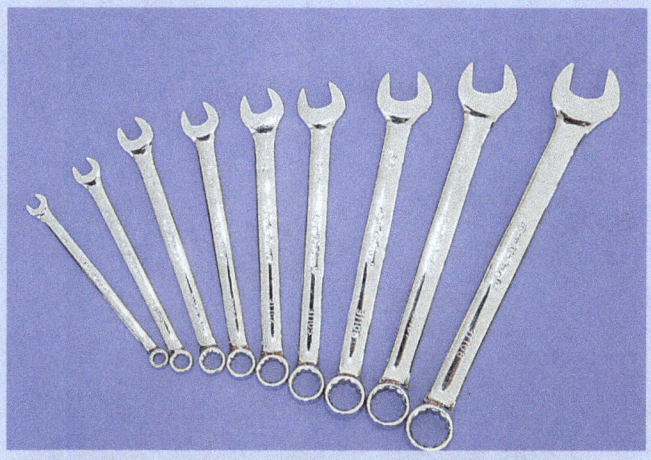

Your tool set needs to include a good set of combination wrenches.

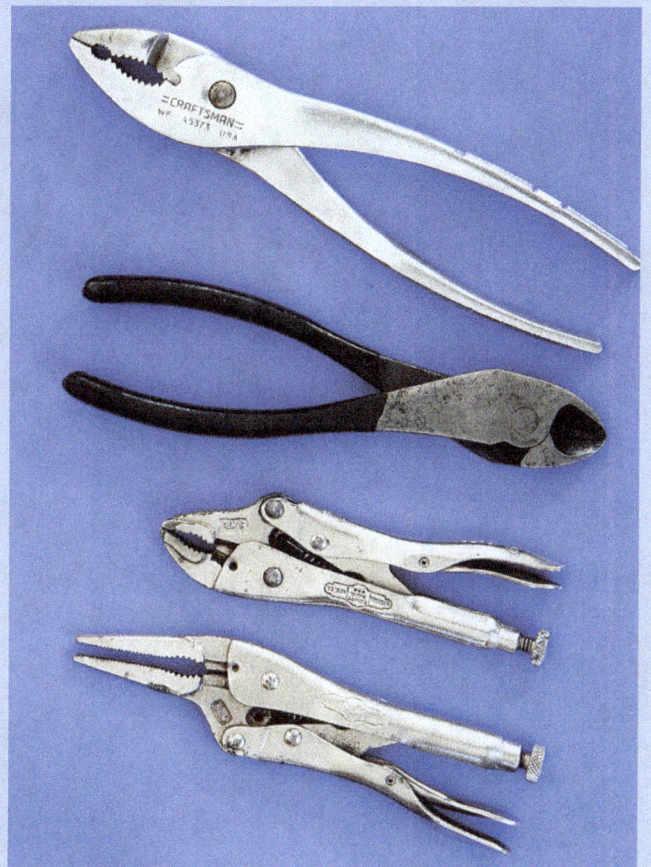

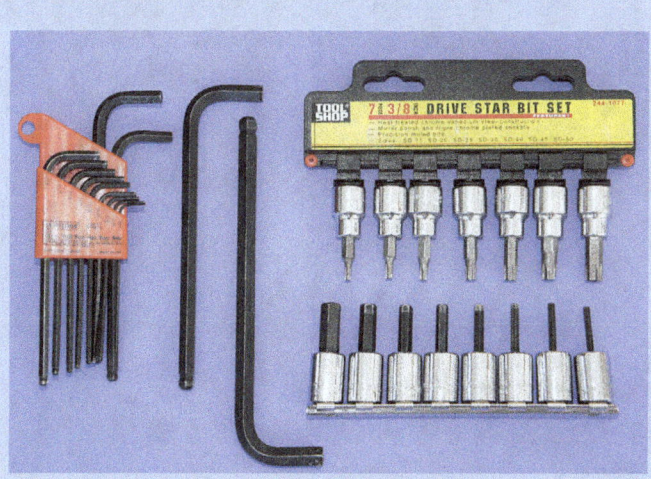

For repairing American motorcycles, you need Allen wrenches and a good set of Torx bits.

It's hard to have too many pairs of pliers, this is jus a starting point.

Chapter Three

Brakes

You Gotta Whoa as well as Go

HOW IT WORKS

Though older motorcycles used mechanical drum brakes, we will only visit the hydraulic disc brake systems. Disc brakes have evolved from a single-piston caliper with organic brake pads matched up to a 10 inch rotor; to a four-piston caliper with semi-metallic pads mated to two, 11.5 inch rotors. The dual four-piston calipers used on the front of many modern Harley-Davidsons provide more stopping power with lighter lever effort

It does not get any more important than this, always look at your brakes for discoloration, rust, leaks, etc. If the brakes are not working properly, look for problems and make repairs.

16

than the older single-piston systems. All brake systems need periodic servicing. The first thing to check on your hydraulic brakes is the condition and level of the fluid. Be sure to check the fluid's color, if the fluid becomes dirty or contaminated it should be flushed with fresh fluid.

Pads need to be replaced when there's about one-third of the pad material left. They should be replaced sooner rather than later to avoid a metal-to-metal condition, which will destroy the rotor's surface. The pad should also be replaced if they become contaminated with grease, brake fluid or dirt.

Brake rotors need to be replaced if any of the following occur: They become worn to the point where they are thinner than the manufacturer's specified minimum thickness, (this spec is often stamped on the rotor or found in the service manual). The rotors have been overheated and have a surface that is cracked, discolored blue/brown, or damaged because the pads were worn to the point of being metal on metal. The brakes pulse or shudder, indicating excessive runout.

Brakes are the most important safety component on any vehicle. On a motorcycle you have no protection from other vehicles or road hazards. It only makes good sense to maintain your brakes and keep them in good working order.

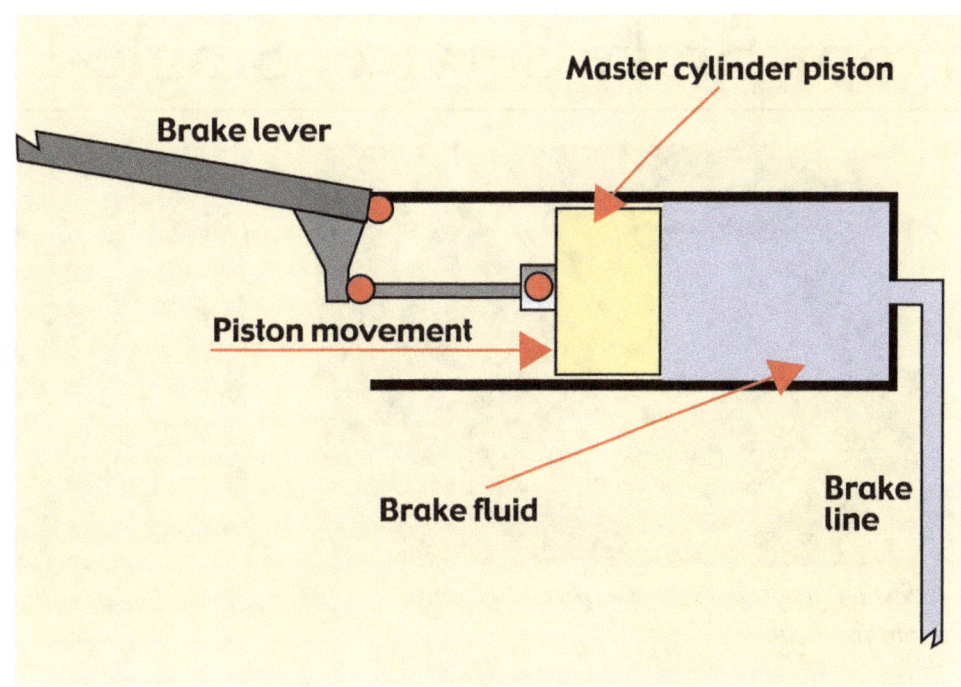

When you pull on the brake lever, the master cylinder piston forces brake fluid out through the brake line to the caliper.

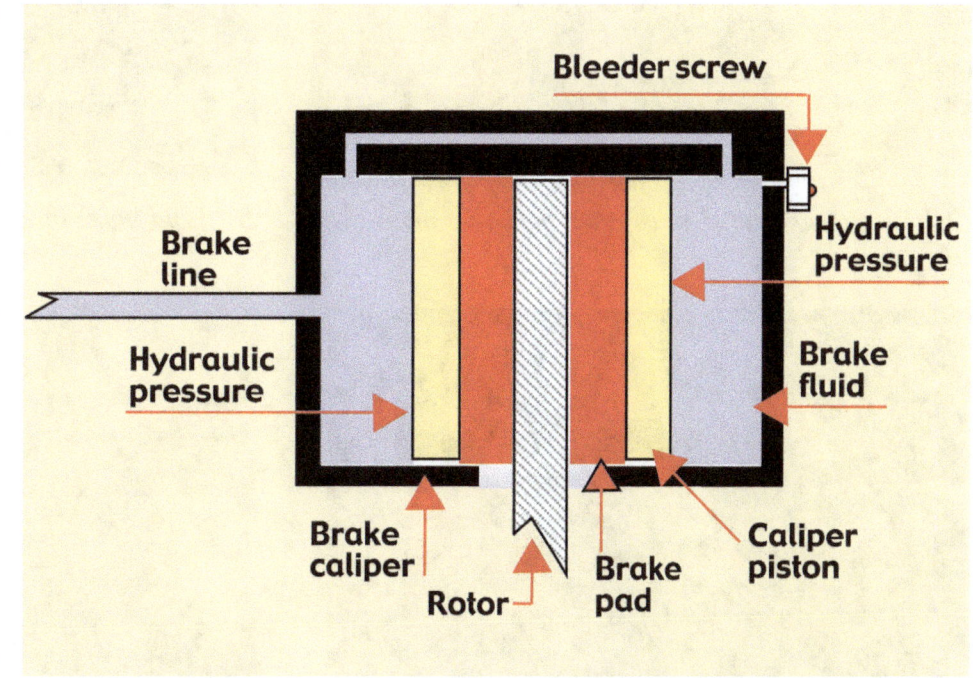

The hydraulic pressure created in the master cylinder forces the caliper pistons toward each other, which in turn forces the brake pads up against the spinning rotor. Though most H-D calipers have 4 pistons, all the principles are the same. The bleeder screw is at the highest point to make it easy to "bleed" out any air in the system.

Front Brake Service, Single-Piston Caliper

1. Shown here is a 1999 or earlier FLH, single piston front caliper.

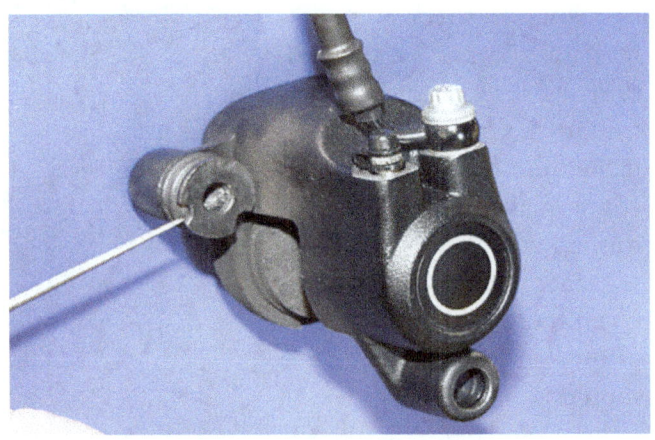

4. We like to pull out the threaded bushing...

2. To start, take out the two Allen bolts that mount the caliper.

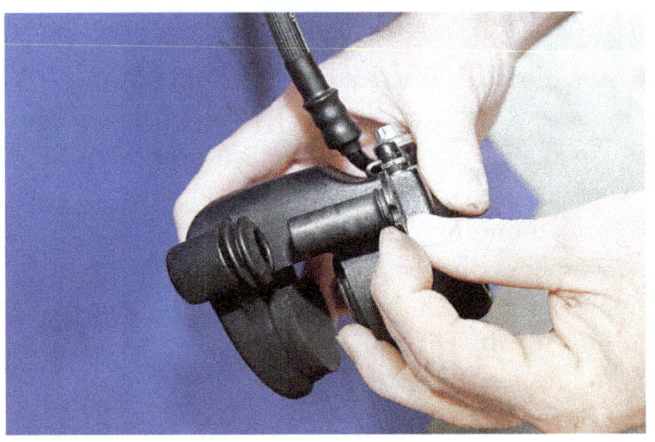

5. ...and make sure it's clean before reassembly.

3. With the 2 mounting bolts removed, slide the caliper backward off the brake rotor.

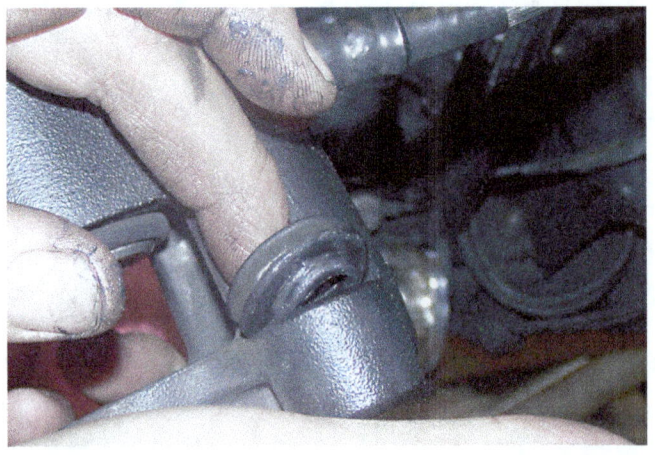

6. Remove the caliper threaded bushing pin boot. Make sure the caliper mounting holes are clean and O-rings are in good shape.

1. Check the pin boot for any holes or dirt, and clean with brake cleaner.

4. Lube the threaded bushing after cleaning, a synthetic brake grease is best.

2. Reinstall the boot and lube the inside of the dust boot.

5. Reassemble the threaded bushing and boot.

3. Clean, inspect and lube the caliper O-rings on lower mount.

6. On the back side, remove the retaining screw for the inboard brake pad and then the pad itself.

19

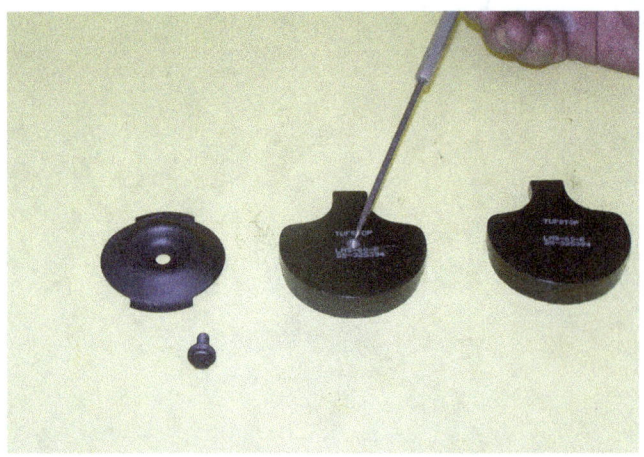

1. The new pad set includes the inboard pad, which is threaded. Put blue Loctite on the retaining screw.

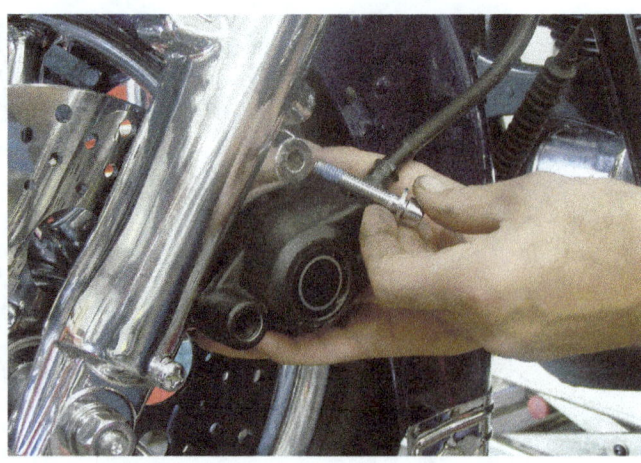

4. Now slide the caliper over the rotor. Install upper mounting screw to hold the caliper in place. Use blue Loctite on the threads.

2. Clean, inspect and lube the spring clip and pad holder. Make sure the threads in the lower caliper mounting hole (arrow) are in good shape and not stripped.

5. Put Loctite on the threaded part of the lower mounting bolt. Lube the slide part of the bolt, and tighten the two mounting bolts evenly to 25 to 30 ft. lbs.

3. Reinstall the pad holder onto the caliper. Make sure you line up the rivet (arrow) with the collar on the threaded bushing.

6. Pump the lever to seat the pads up against the rotor, this **must** be done prior to the first road test or you will have no brakes on the first application. Injury or death may result.

The 4-piston caliper shown here was used on 2000 to 2007 models.

With a 1/4 inch, 12 point socket crack the pad retaining bolts prior to caliper removal.

1. Loosen the two caliper mounting bolts. They are 10mm, with 12 point heads.

4. Push the brake pistons back into the caliper with a large pry bar or flat tip screwdriver.

2. Hold the caliper when removing second bolt so it won't fall and hit the fender.

5. Now remove the brake pad retaining pins

3. The caliper's off and ready for brake pad replacement. Wash the caliper pistons with Brake Kleen and blow off with compressed air prior to pushing the pads back into the caliper.

6. The brake retaining pins and 1/4 inch, 12 point socket. Check the pins for wear and replace as needed.

1. The brake pads will drop out after the pins are removed.

4. Install the inside pad, it has a larger ear on the top, and push it up against the anti-rattle spring.

2. Slide the outboard pad in place. The pads are not the same and go in only one way.

5. With your thumb push the pad up against the spring as you push the back pin into place.

3. With the pad in place, you must push it up against the anti-rattle spring. Then slide the retaining pin in to hold it in place.

6. Screw the pins down until seated. Torque after the caliper in mounted

1. Slide the caliper over the rotor, be careful not to scratch the fender.

4. Torque the caliper mounting hardware to 28 to 38 ft. lbs. Torque the pad retaining bolts to 180 to 200 in. lbs.

2. Use blue Loctite on the threads.

3. Screw the mounting bolts in through mounts in lower slider and tighten.

5. Pump the brake lever to seat pads against the rotor. The brake pads must be seated - injury or death can occur if pads are not seated.

Late-Model Front Pad Replacement

1. Typical 2008 FLHT front brake caliper setup.

4. Pull the retaining clip from the pad retaining pin.

2. Remove the 10mm, 12 point caliper bolts.

5. Using a 5mm Allen wrench, loosen the pin.

3. Now pull the screw from the caliper body.

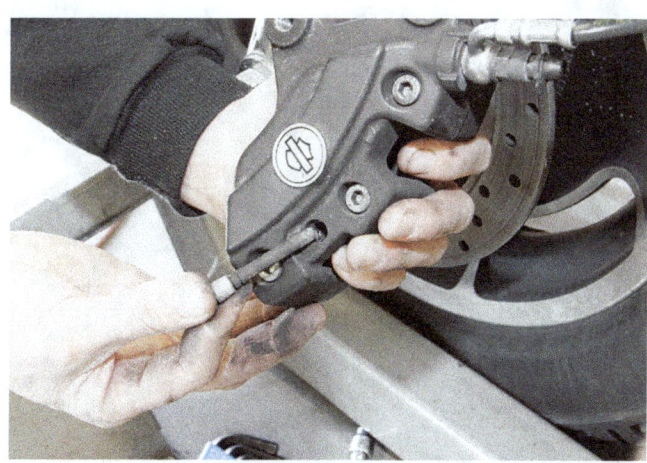

6. Pull the pin from the pads. Wash with Brake Kleen and blow off with compressed air (not shown).

1. Push the pistons back into the caliper body with a large screwdriver.

4. Reinstall the anti-rattle spring - after cleaning the spring and pushing the brake pistons back into the caliper.

2. Lift the inner and outer brake pads from the caliper.

5. Install the new inboard pad as shown.

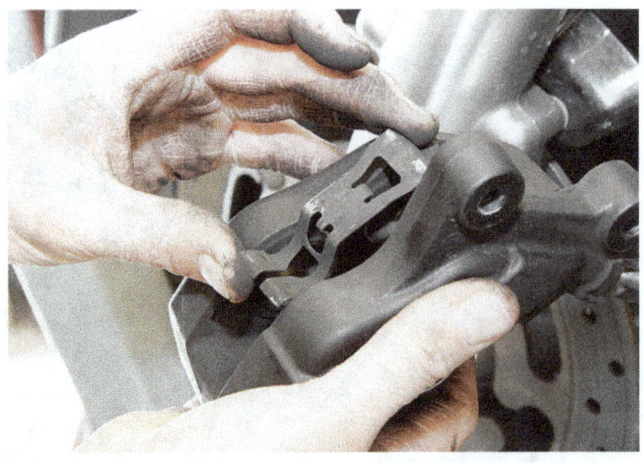

3. Inspect and clean the anti-rattle spring. The forked end of the spring goes toward the brake retaining pin end.

6. Install the outboard pad...

1. ...You will have to push both pads against the anti-rattle spring in order to slide the brake retaining pin into place.

4. Push the screen-prongs under the end of the anti-rattle spring and snap the screen into place.

2. Screw in the retaining pin and torque it to 75 to 102 in. lbs.

5. Slide the caliper over the rotor. Be careful not to scratch the fender, there isn't much clearance.

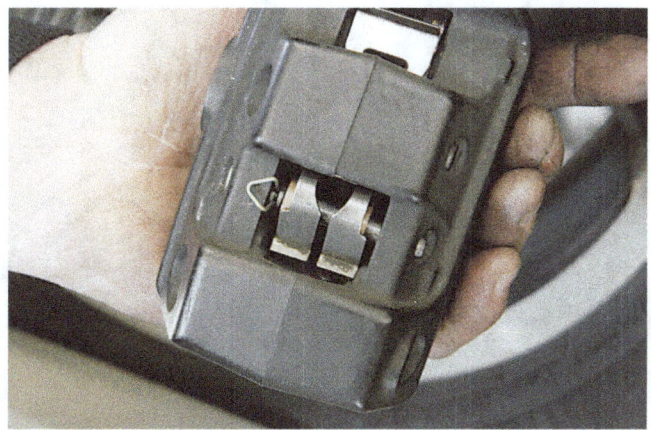

3. This is what the assembled caliper - with pads, spring, and retaining pin with lock clip - looks like.

6. Use blue Loctite on the mounting bolts, and tighten to 28 to 30 ft. lbs. **Pump the brake lever to seat the pads, prior to riding.** Injury or death can result if you don't pump up the lever.

Break Pads

Brake pads can be manufactured from different materials, and for most popular bikes there are two types of pads: those that contain metal and those that don't.

Metallic pads wear well and provide good stopping power, but they can score the surface of polished rotors. These are sometimes called sintered iron pads, examples of these pads can be seen below.

Non-metallic pads are often called organic, these pads no longer use any asbestos. Today they are manufactured from Kevlar or other high temperature fibers mixed with a resin. These organic pads are softer and will not cut the surface of those nice polished rotors.

As a rule of thumb in our shop, for factory bikes with stock rotors we prefer to use the sintered pads. They last longer and grab the rotor better. But if the bike has polished rotors, then we go with a set of the organic pads.

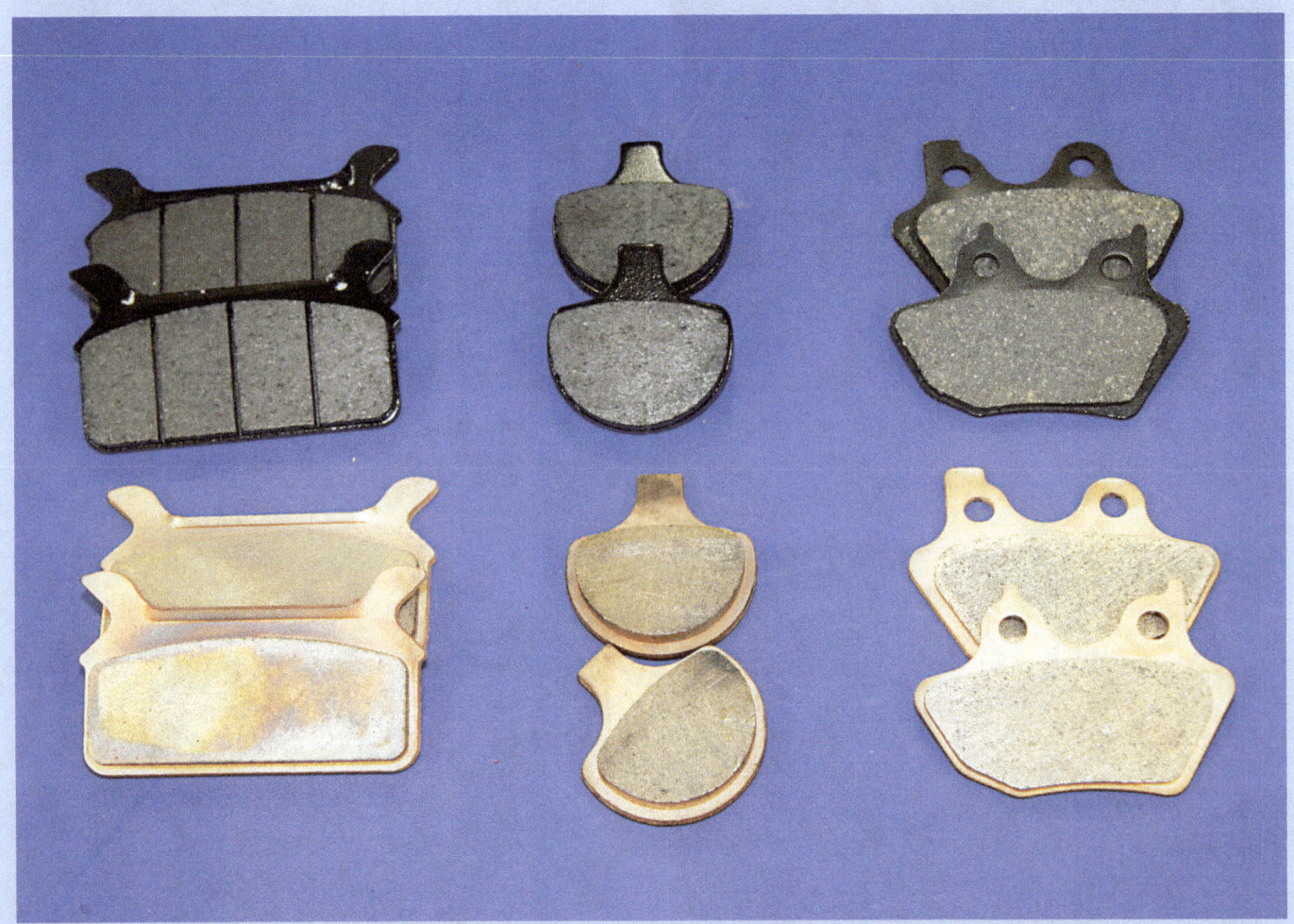

Most popular brake pads are available in both metallic and non-metallic pad compounds. Which one you choose depends on rotor material and finish. If in doubt, ask the counter person at your local shop for help.

Rear Brake Pad Replacement

Putting brake pads in the rear of a bike, especially a Bagger, can seem like a hassle. In most cases though, it's just a little extra work to get some of the other parts out of the way so you can get at the caliper and the pads. With the late model Bagger seen here, we took off one muffler, and the railings that wrap around the right side saddle bag.

The four piston caliper on the back of the Bagger was used on the rear of many Harley-Davidsons from 2000 up to 2005, the thing to remember here is that you do not have to remove the caliper to remove the pads. You do have to remove the two pad retaining bolts, and then the pads can be slipped out from between the caliper and the rotor.

In order to pull the pads out from the caliper, you have to push the pistons back into the caliper. Before pushing the pistons back into the caliper though, we like to clean out the area behind the brake pad (note the nearby photos). We do this so dirt on the pistons does not hang up the piston, or mar the piston's sealing surface as they are pushed back into the bore. The rest of the job is pretty simple. Note that the inner and outer pad are not the same. Be sure to pump up the bake pedal before you go for the first ride.

Rear brake pads in bikes using the caliper shown here can be serviced without removal of the caliper.

Wash the old pads and pistons with Brake Kleen, and blow off with compressed air, before pushing the pistons back into their bores.

Push the piston back in to the caliper bore. Use a large flat-tip screwdriver.

1. Push the inboard pad into the back side of the caliper body.

4. The brake pads will slide down, note the pads are different.

2. Loosen 1/4 inch, 12 point brake pad retaining pins.

5. Remove the inboard pad. It will slide out or fall out.

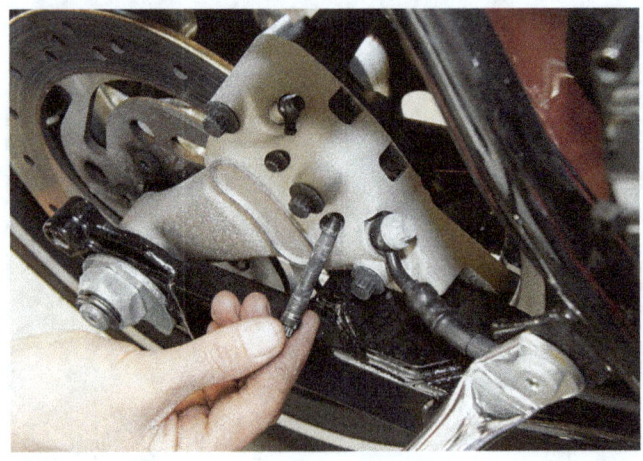

3. Remove the two brake pad pins.

6. Slide the new pads into place. Note the different pad top ears between the inboard and outboard pads.

1. Push the pad upward and slip the pad retaining pin into pad to hold in position.

4. With both pads in place, tighten the pad retaining pins into the caliper body.

2. Install the inboard pad. Push up on the pad and slide the rear pin in.

5. Torque the pad retaining pins to 180 to 200 in. lbs. (15 to 17 ft. lbs.).

3. Using a screwdriver, push the pad up into the spring the and slide front pin into the caliper.

6. Pump the brake pedal to seat the pads. Caution: don't forget to seat the pads. Serious bodily injury or death can occur if bypassed.

Rotor Service

To check for rotor runout without special tools, you can make a pointer from a gas-welding rod. Attach it as shown.

Make a ninety degree bend in the pointer and position as shown. Be sure the pointer is rigid.

Heat is the enemy of rotors. When you pull the bike down from 80 or more miles per hour, all that energy converts to heat. In some cases, or over time, the heat causes the metal rotors to change shape or warp.

Unlike automotive rotors, which can often be resurfaced to make them flat again, there just isn't enough material on a motorcycle rotor to allow for the removal of any metal. If motorcycle rotors are warped, there is only one answer, replacement.

Most replacement motorcycle rotors are made from stainless steel. Some are polished. If your bike is a stock Bagger or Softail, you might just want a set of rotors from the dealer or local shop.

The service manuals show mechanics checking the rotors with a dial indicator, a specialized tool you may not have in the garage. Shown here is a method for checking the runout of a rotor with nothing more elaborate than a piece of welding rod and a set of feeler gauges. The important thing is to be sure the pointer is stable and rigid so the two readings are accurate. Any rotor with more than .008 inches of runout will cause the lever to pulsate on a hard stop, and should be replaced. Use Loctite on the rotor-mounting fasteners and torque to factory specs.

Rotate the rotor to the position where the pointer is closest to the rotor, and measure that distance with a feeler gauge.

1. Now rotate to the position where the pointer is farthest away from the rotor and measure again. The Difference between the two readings is runout. Any rotor with more than .008 inches of runout should be replaced.

2. An impact wrench works well to break the rotor-mounting bolts loose. These fasteners can strip easily so be sure the tool is fully seated in the bolt before you attempt removal.

3. Install the new rotor on clean hub surface. Make sure you line up all 5 bolt holes. Start all mounting bolts before you begin tightening.

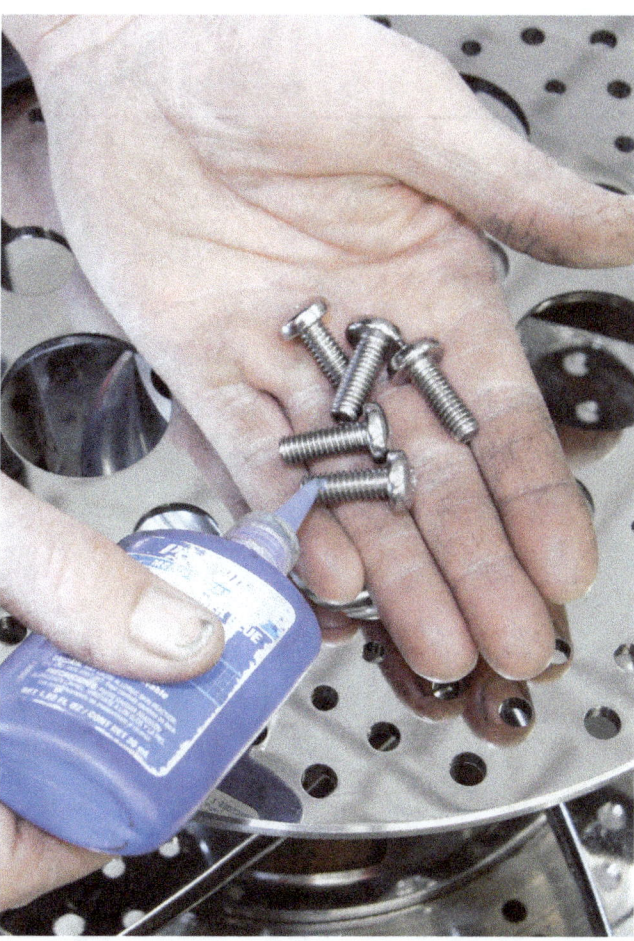

4. Use blue Loctite on the mounting bolts. Be sure the threads in the hub are clean before the bolts are installed. If in doubt, chase the threads with a tap.

5. Torque the 5 mounting bolts in a cross pattern. Tighten the front rotor mounting bolts evenly to 16 to 24 ft. lbs.

Bleed the Brakes

Most American-made V-twins use either DOT 4 or DOT 5 brake fluid. Be sure to read the master cylinder cap to determine which fluid is correct for the bike. Do not mix the two as they are NOT compatible.

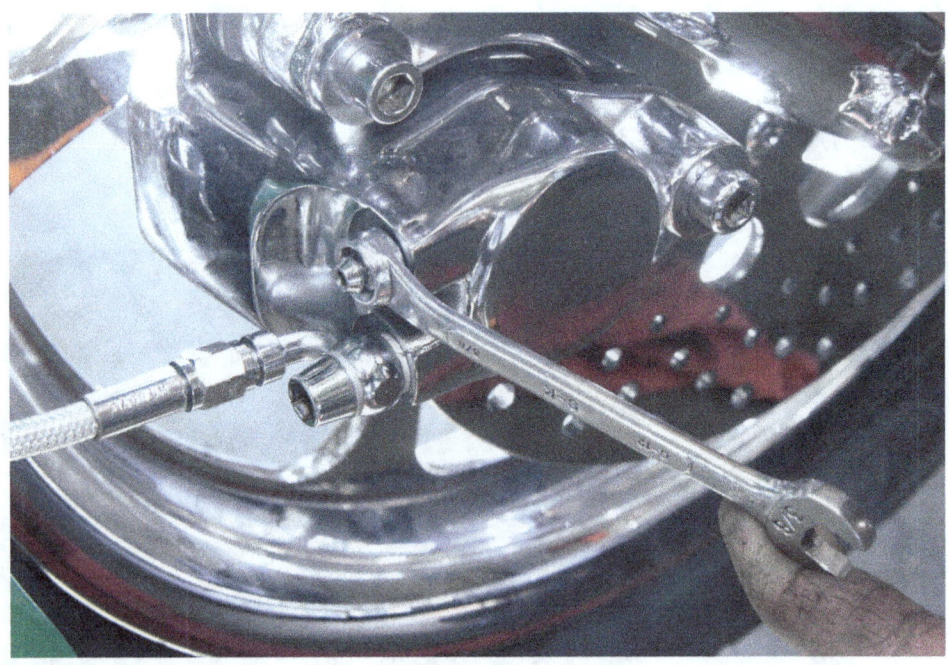

Make sure the six-point box wrench is square on the bleeder screw before you loosen. And be careful not to over-tighten, as they can easily strip.

When it comes to bleeding brakes on a bike, we like to back-bleed the brakes. There are tools and pumps made just for this job, but we like to use a pump oil can and a piece of vacuum hose.

The idea is to open the bleeder valve at the caliper, attach the pump and force clean brake fluid up into the caliper and up through the line to the master cylinder. Ideally all the air in the system is pushed out of the system ahead of the brake fluid.

Be sure that the fluid you use is the same fluid, DOT 4 or DOT 5, that was used in the bike originally. The two fluids are chemically very different and do not mix well.

Sometimes, even after the master cylinder is full of fluid, the lever will be a little spongy. To eliminate any little air bubbles that may be lingering in the master cylinder, simply pump the lever back and forth a number of times. As you do so, tiny bubbles may be seen rising to the top of the reservoir.

To eliminate any air left in the caliper, hold moderate pressure on the lever, then open the bleeder screw. If what comes out of the bleeder is a froth of fluid and air, you need to repeat the process until only pure fluid leaves the bleeder. Be sure to close the bleeder before you take the pressure off the lever, or you will suck air back into the caliper.

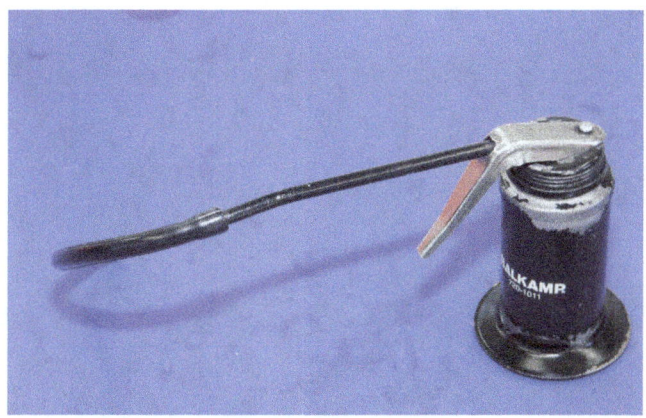

1. When back-bleeding the brakes make sure the oil can you use is totally clean and free of any oil residue. It's best to have a dedicated oil can for bleeding. Use a piece of vacuum hose between the can and bleeder.

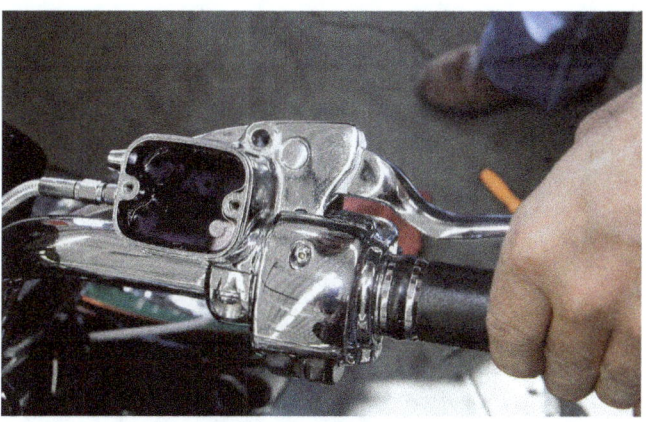

4. Pump the brake lever a few times to check that the lever feels solid. Be careful not to pump the lever too fast or hard because fluid will shoot out of the top of the master cylinder. Any air left in the system will create a soft or spongy feeling lever.

2. Pump all the air out of the hose and attach to the open bleeder.

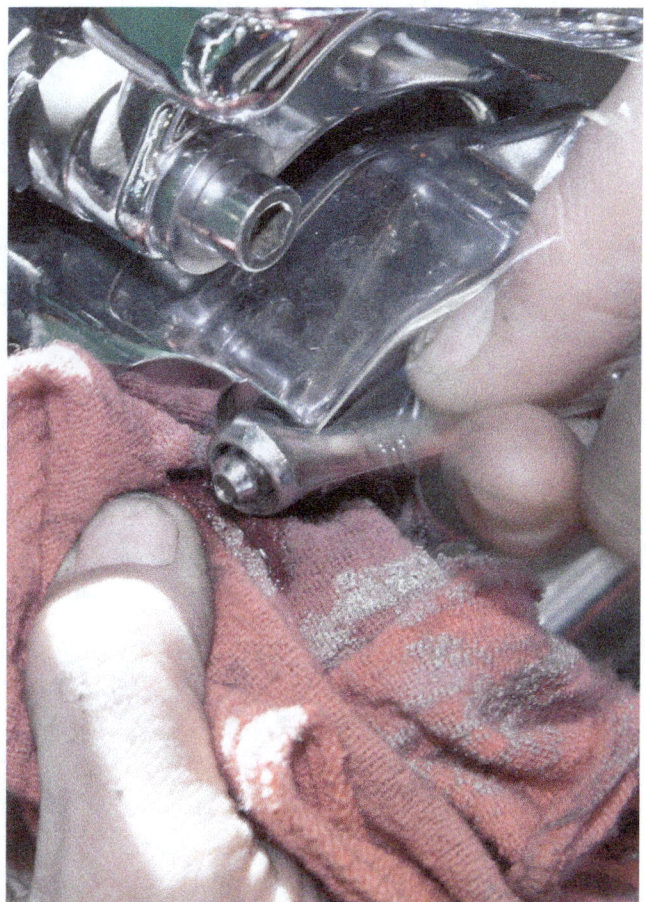

3. When back bleeding brakes, make sure the master cylinder is clean. Pump the oil can and watch the reservoir for air bubbles. Close the bleeder when the bubbles stop and you have pure brake fluid coming into the master.

5. As a final check you can hold mild pressure on the lever, then open the bleeder screw. Only fluid and no air should come out of the bleeder. Be sure to close the bleeder before you let up the pressure on the lever or air will be drawn back into the caliper.

Chapter Four

The Primary Drive

Chains, Sprockets and Clutches

THE PRIMARY DRIVE IS MADE UP OF FOUR COMPONENTS:

1. Primary chain. The primary chain connects the engine and transmission. The chain and sprockets have a lot to do with the bike's gearing. The gear ratio can be changed by changing the front sprocket. The primary drive does require maintenance. The oil needs to be changed and the chain needs to be adjusted to the proper tension. If the primary chain is too tight, the clutch won't release. If it's too loose it will clang and bang. What gets the fluid dirty is the clutch. If the oil is black, it's because the clutch is going away.

2. Compensator sprocket assembly. The com-

The typical primary drive consisting of 4 major components: 1.Clutch & hub assembly 2. Primary drive chain which connects the motor to the transmission main shaft. Slack adjuster (aka, the shoe), used to adjust chain tension. 3. Compensator sprocket which helps absorb motor pulsations.

pensator assembly is splined to the engine shaft, this component includes a heavy spring and a set of ramps that take a lot of the chugging out of the drive. The sprocket assembly absorbs the pulsations from the motor. Without the compensator sprocket they chug more, and they pulsate at certain speeds, and some of the shock is transmitted to the chain.

3. Clutch. The clutch can be engaged or disengaged. When engaged, the power of the engine is delivered to the transmission. When disengaged, the primary chain runs, but none of that power is delivered to the transmission. Incorporated on the clutch hub is the ring gear for the starter. For most applications you can change out the ring gear without replacing the whole clutch hub.

4. The chain adjuster. There are two types of adjusters in common use. The automatic adjuster, found on all the 6 speed bikes, requires no adjusting. If the chain gets too old, however, past the specification for that bike, it will have to be replaced because there isn't enough movement in the adjuster to compensate for a chain that's essentially worn out. The manual adjuster, or primary shoe, is found on all 2006 and earlier bikes.

2006 and older bikes require that you open the inspection door, turn the motor over to find the tightest spot in the chain, and then adjust the chain tension by moving the shoe up or down. There should be about 5/8 to 7/8 inch of up and down movement with the engine cold. Normally, the shoe itself doesn't show much wear, but if you run low on lubricant you might need to replace the shoe because then the chain will cut into the material. When you replace the shoe, be sure you install it the right way (check the nearby photos). When it comes to lubricant, we like to use the Syn 3 oil right from the beginning in the primary housing. By the way, Sportsters use a common oil for the primary and transmission. Big twins use separate oil for the transmission and the primary.

Service the primary every 2500 miles, do it when you change oil, if the magnet on the plug is fill of metal, then pull the outer cover and do a complete inspection of all the components, the starter gear too. When you service the derby cover consider the new round gasket, it works better than the old O-ring.

A clean work area is always helpful to any job. Drain the fluid from the rear lower corner of primary drive prior to dismantling.

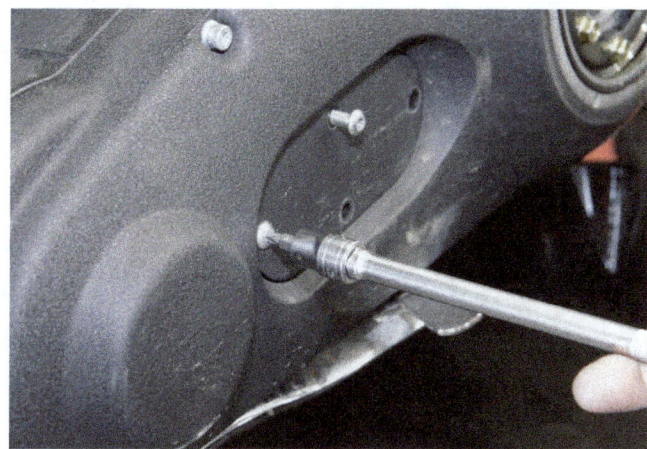

The inspection cover must be removed. The screws go through into the inner cover.

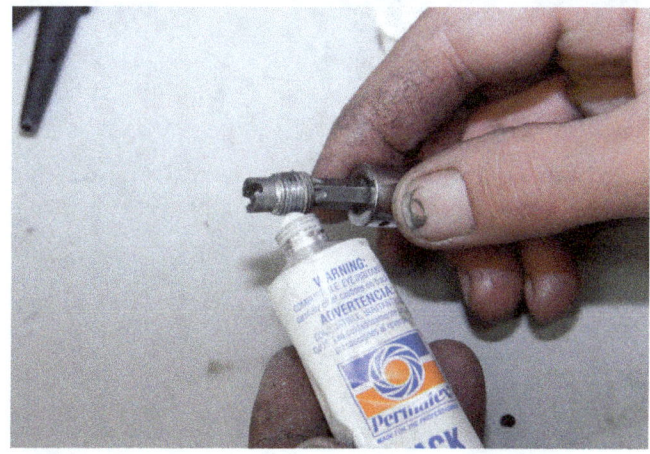

Clean the drain plug magnet. Before reinstalling, always use thread sealant on all drain plugs.

37

1. The primary drive with the outer cover off prior to disassembly. Be sure to look for metal and fiber debris.

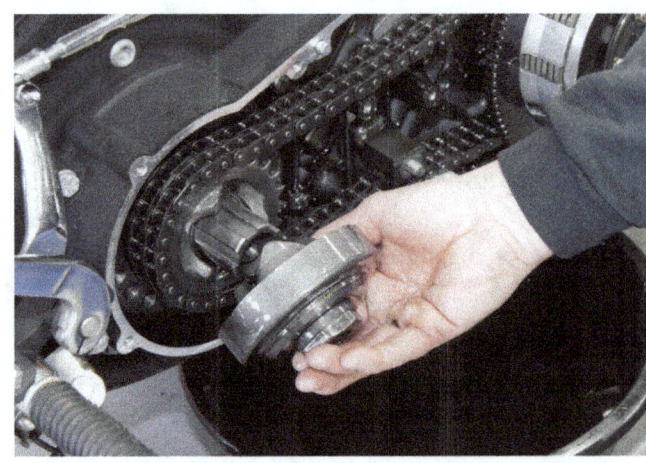

4. Now take off the outer compensator, tension spring, and ramp. The ramp is splined to the inner motor sprocket shaft.

2. Take the nut off completely from the primary chain shoe/slack adjuster.

5. Loosen the lock nut for the clutch adjustment, and back off the adjustment.

3. Remove the engine sprocket compensator with an impact gun.

6. Remove the snap-ring from clutch hub with a snap ring pliers.

1. With the snap ring out of the way, the clutch adjustment plate and adjusting screw can be removed.

4. The clutch hub assembly and engine sprocket slides off the motor and transmission shafts as an assembly.

2. The clutch hub nut is a left-handed thread and must be turned clockwise to remove.

5. The inner primary housing with only the inner sprocket shaft extension and the alternator assembly still in place.

3. The shoulder nut for the clutch-hub-to-transmission main shaft is left-handed. Check the condition of the nut and replace if damaged or distorted.

6. This is the inner sprocket shaft extension being removed from the engine shaft. Don't lose this shim, it is used to align the primary chain between the engine and transmission sprockets.

The Clutch

Shown is a complete, late-model clutch assembly. The starter motor engages the outer ring of teeth (the ring gear) to turn over the engine.

Here we begin the disassembly of the clutch by removing the top pressure plate ring. This is a late-model Twin Cam assembly, earlier models are slightly different, be sure to check your service manual for details.

How it works

When you pull on the cable the ball-and-ramp assembly - under the right side transmission cover - moves the clutch pushrod against the pressure plate. The pressure plate moves against the pressure of the clutch spring, effectively releasing the clutch. When you release the lever, the pushrod moves away from the pressure plate and the pressure of the clutch spring is applied to the clutch discs. Note: in 2006 the ball-and-ramp assembly was changed to ease the clutch pull, and these later assemblies can be used in the earlier bikes.

Service

It's important to keep the correct amount of free play. If you don't have enough free play it's like having the clutch not fully engaged, the full pressure of the clutch spring can't be applied to the clutch discs. The factory clutch on newer bikes uses a light spring, for light hand pressure. If you do any performance work on the motor you need to put in a better spring so the clutch can handle the extra power. Putting in a stiffer spring is the single easiest way to upgrade the clutch.

The clutch assembly is made up of a clutch hub that contains a stack of alternating discs made of either steel or fiber. Disassembly and assembly of the clutch assembly is shown nearby.

Under the right side transmission cover there is the clutch release bearing. After 20,000 miles you should inspect this bearing.

The Clutch

1. With the top screws removed we pull off the spring retainer (in his right hand) and diaphragm spring.

4. This inner dampener spring seat helps soften engagement and release.

2. The clutch assembly dismantled, the steel and fiber plate are staggered: fiber, then steel, then fiber again.

5. All clutch plates are not the same. The inner fiber plate is narrower.

3. The last "disc" to come out is the inner dampener spring seat.

6. Reassembly: Start by assembling the clutch fiber and steel discs in to a staggered pack. The fiber plates have ears that engage with the outer hub.

The Clutch

1. The "teeth" on the steel plates engage into matching recesses in the inner hub.

4. You can see how the diaphragm spring is aligned onto the inner hub.

2. Lube all clutch plates prior to assembly, use primary oil or Synthetic 3 lubricant. New fiber plates need to be soaked in the oil before assembly.

5. Use blue Loctite on the plate screws.

3. Time to install the pressure plate, which maintains pressure on the fiber and steel plates.

6. Tighten down plate screws in a staggered pattern, then torque to manufacturer's specifications. In this case 90 to 110 in. lbs.

1. To start the re-assembly, install the clutch assembly and motor sprocket with the primary chain onto the transmission and engine shafts.

2. Slide the chain slack tensioner (or shoe) onto its mounting bolt as you slide the chain and sprocket into place.

3. At this point we have the clutch, motor sprocket and chain tensioner in place.

4. Use red Loctite on the clutch hub nut. Clean away dirt and oil from the shaft nut with solvent before assembly.

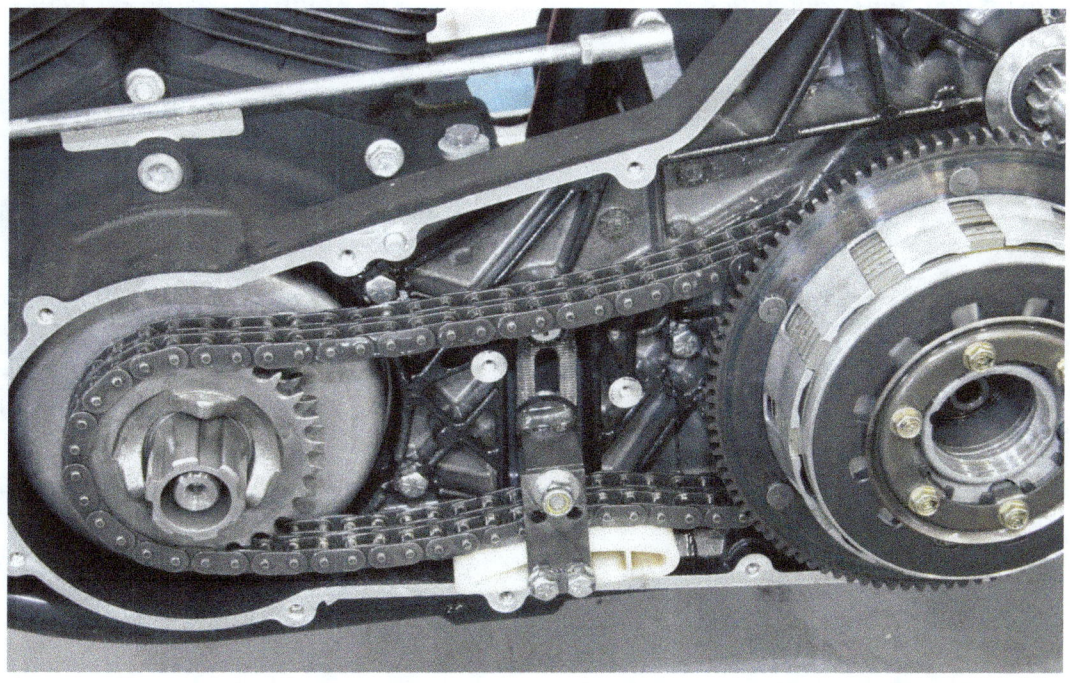

1. Next, install the main-shaft to the clutch-hub nut. Remember that it is a left-handed thread.

4. Install the outer compensator ramp on the engine shaft extension.

2. Lock the hub with a lock tool before torquing the engine and clutch-hub nuts.

5. Clean the motor sprocket threads and nut with cleaner or solvent, then put Loctite on the compensator sprocket nut.

3. Torque the clutch hub nut to 70 - 80 ft. lbs.

6. Install the compensator sprocket and torque to 150 to 165 ft. lbs.

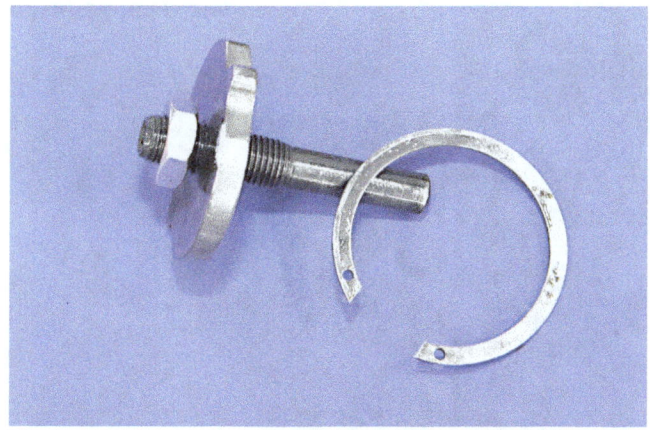

1. The clutch release plate with the adjusting screw, lock nut, and the snap ring that holds it in place. The adjusting screw contacts the clutch pushrod inside the transmission main shaft.

2. Slide the release plate and adjusting screw assembly into the clutch hub. Before installation, lube the inside tip of the adjusting screw with white lube.

3. Use a snap-ring pliers to install the snap ring, be sure the ring snaps fully into the groove in the clutch-hub.

4. Loosen the jam nut on the cable slack adjuster and adjust it so there is a large amount of play at the cable/lever.

5. Set the initial clutch adjustment: Screw the adjusting screw in until it is lightly seated against the clutch pushrod, then back off 1/2 to 1 turn and tighten the jam nut to 70 to 120 in. lbs.

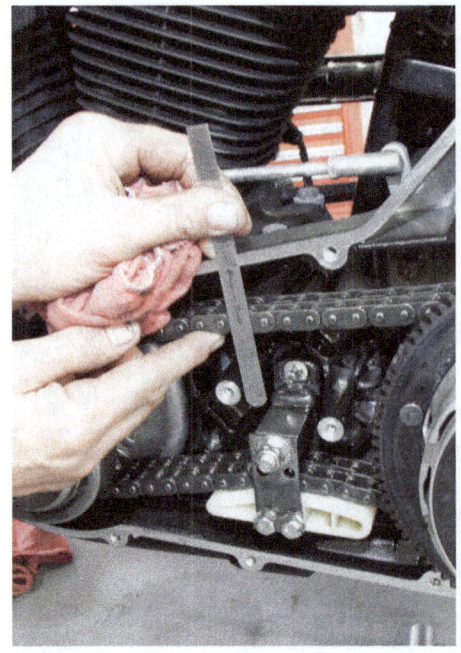  

1. Adjust the primary chain at the tightest spot (rotate the motor to find the tightest spot). With the motor cold, set the play at 5/8 to 7/8 inch of up and down movement. Tighten the nut on the primary shoe bolt to 21-29 ft. lbs.

2. Next, check the chain alignment between the two sprockets. Here we are measuring the distance from the straightedge to the case-edge at the front.

3. Now we make the same measurement at the rear, the two measurements should be within .030 inches. If the measurement is too far out of specification, the shim under the sprocket shaft extension should be changed to move the compensator sprocket assembly in or out.

4. After cleaning off all the gasket material, clean the parting surface and wipe it down with solvent.

5. Don't forget the inner primary center gaskets. Always use new gaskets when installing the primary cover.

1. Install the outer primary, lightly tighten the screws in a cross pattern, then torque to 108 to 120 in. lbs.

4. Adjust the cable to obtain the correct amount of free play at the lever (see the next photo) and tighten the jam nut. Then slide the boot over the adjuster.

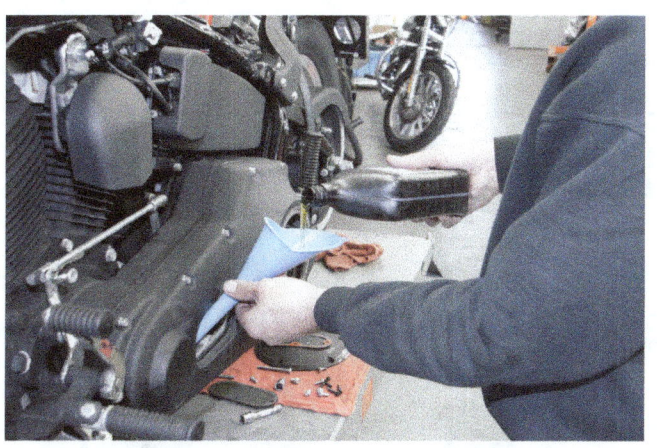

2. Fill the primary housing to the specifications noted in the handbook. Always make sure the lower parts of the chain are immersed in fluid.

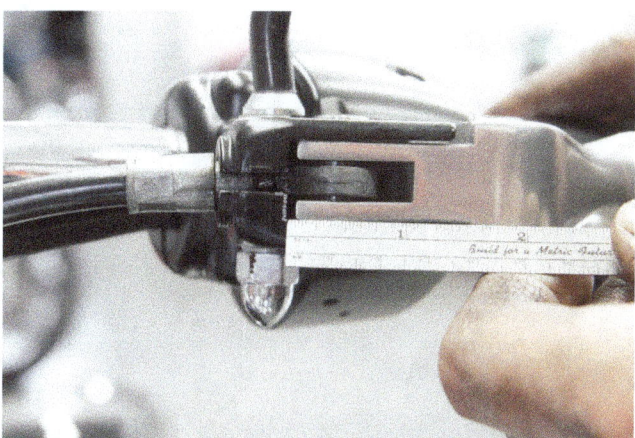

5. Free play, or unloaded play, should be 1/16-1/8 inches as shown. The amount of free play can be set to a particular rider's preference as long as there is at least 1/16 inch.

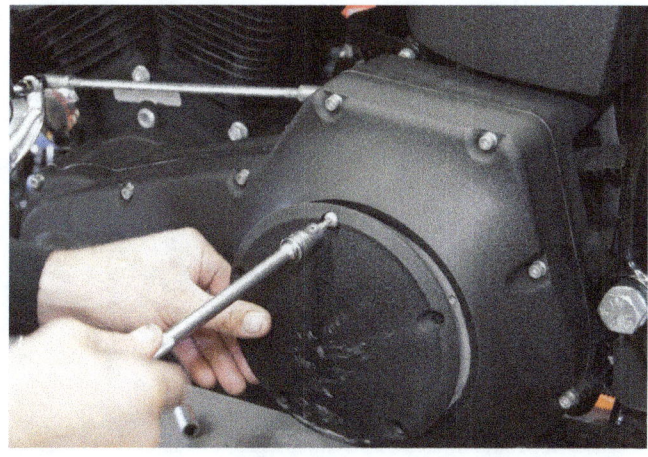

3. Tighten the derby cover screws to 84 to 108 in. lbs. Use a new O-ring, or one of the new gaskets which we recommend.

6. After reassembly and a road test, check for leaks and clutch operation.

47

Chapter Five

Electrical

Charging Circuit, Starter, and Battery

How it Works

The electrical system in your V-twin motorcycle is really pretty simple. The battery provides the initial power to turn the starter, and power the ignition. Once the motor fires, the charging system begins producing power. Power that is used to recharge the battery and run the ignition, lights and any other accessories. If the charging circuit isn't putting out quite enough power to run everything, when you pull up to a light with all the

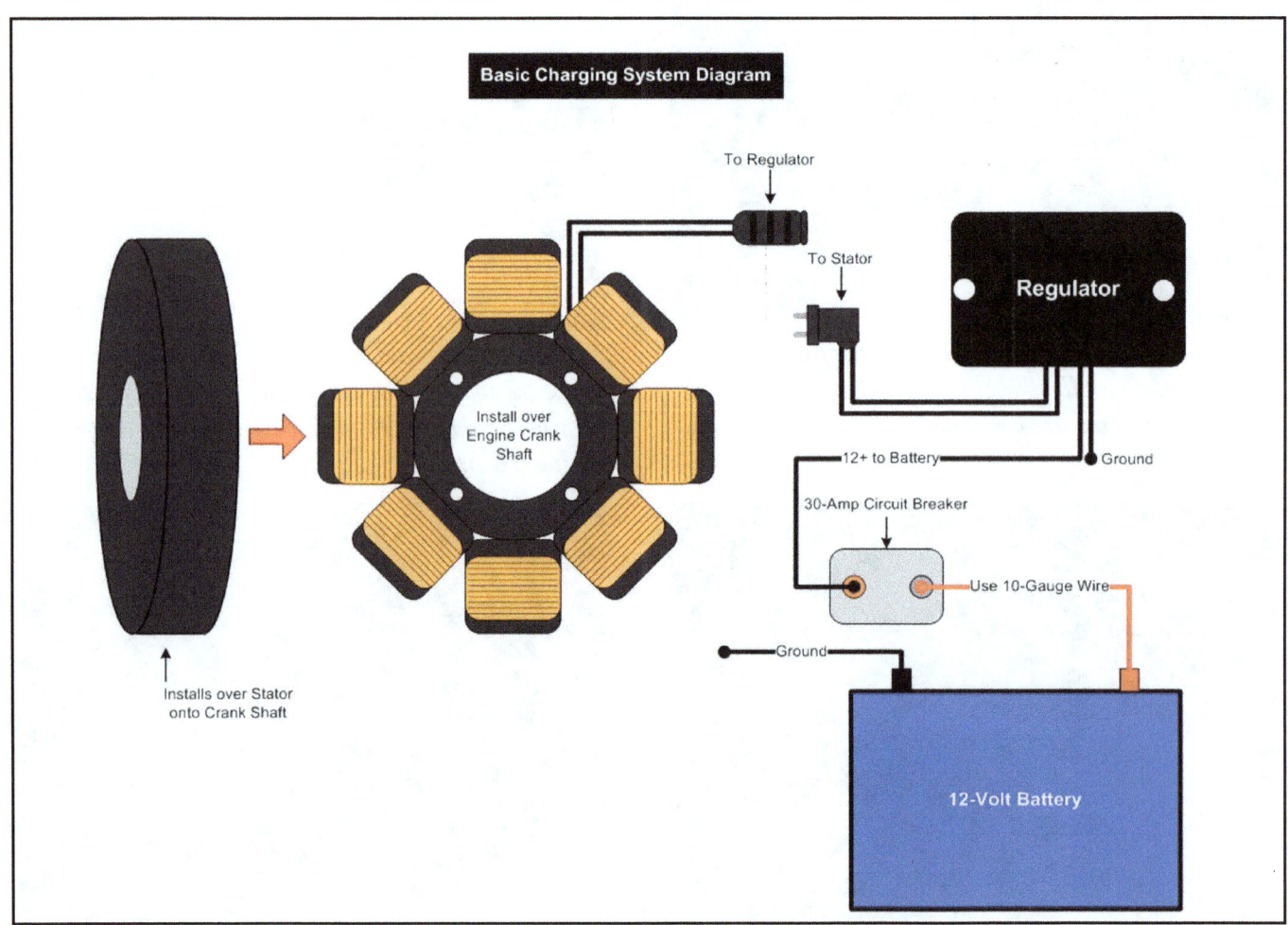

The basic American V-twin charging circuit is actually pretty simple and consists of three basic components: the stator, the rotor, and the regulator. NAMZ

accessories on your Bagger turned on, then the battery will step in with enough power to fill the gap until you twist the throttle and engine speed increases. As the engine spins faster so does the rotor which means more output from the alternator. The power produced by the alternator is actually alternating current (AC). A regulator is used to convert this power to direct current (DC), and keep the voltage in a range that can be used by the motorcycle.

The Alternator

Different bikes have different power requirements. Newer, late model Baggers use a 45 amp or larger charging system, while early bikes might have a system that only puts out 15 amps. When replacing the complete charging system you can upgrade to a larger output system, but when making a repair stay with matching components. Most have a plug connector at the stator that must match the plug on the voltage regulator.

As shown in the diagram (on the left), the alternator is made up of three major components: a stationary stator, a rotor that spins with the engine, and a regulator. Replacing the stator is a fair amount of work so you want to get the diagnosis right the first time. Replacing the stator, and trouble-shooting a problem are explained a few pages farther along.

Alternator R&R

As shown in chapter 3, we start with a disassembled primary and ...

...remove the sprocket shaft extension and shim. Don't lose the shim, they come in different sizes.

With two picks, pull the rotor from the shaft, it will be hard to pull off the shaft because of the heavy magnets on the rotor's outer edge.

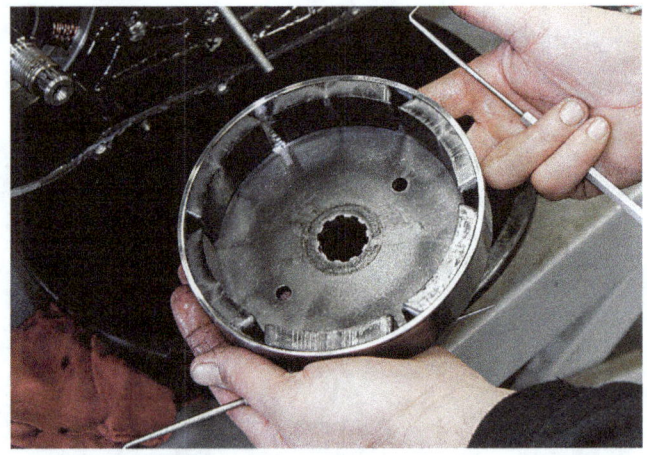

1. Here's a look at the inside of the rotor. Check for loose magnets, and metal chips and debris. Also check the splines for wear.

4. Remove the stator-wire retainer next, it is held in place by two small Phillips screws.

2. The stator assembly is held in place by four, T27 Torx fasteners.

5. Here's the stator-wire retainer.

3. Remove the Torx fasteners, don't reuse these, always install new bolts and torque to the correct specification.

6. Now you can slide the stator off the engine-bearing-cage boss.

1. After disconnecting the plug from the regulator, you have to push the stator plug out through the crankcases.

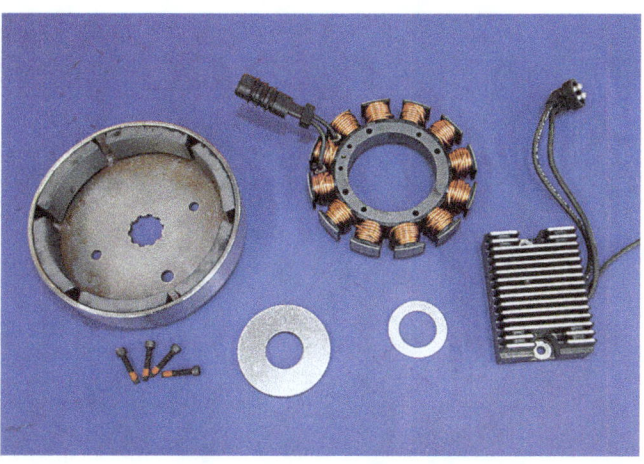

3. We like to replace all the components with a complete charging system kit including the stator, rotor, voltage regulator and necessary hardware

2. Then you can pull out the old stator, which in this case had no A/C voltage output when we did the diagnostic test.

4. Before beginning the reassembly, we apply a small amount of RTV silicone to the alternator plug to help prevent oil leaking past the plug.

5. Here's the new stator going into position.

51

1. Here's the new stator reinstalled with the original inner shim on the shaft.

2. Torque the four new screws to 30 to 40 in. lbs. (in most cases, check your manual). They come with Loctite already applied.

3. Slide the stator plug through the crank cases and reinstall the stator-wire retainer, use blue Loctite on the phillips screws.

4. Install the rotor back on to sprocket shaft, use picks for installation so it does not slam onto the new stator (the magnets will tend to pull it toward the engine).

5. Here the stator and rotor are reinstalled and ready for the primary drive components to be installed, see the primary section.

Regulator R&R

1. The voltage regulator is located on the front of a Softail's lower chassis.

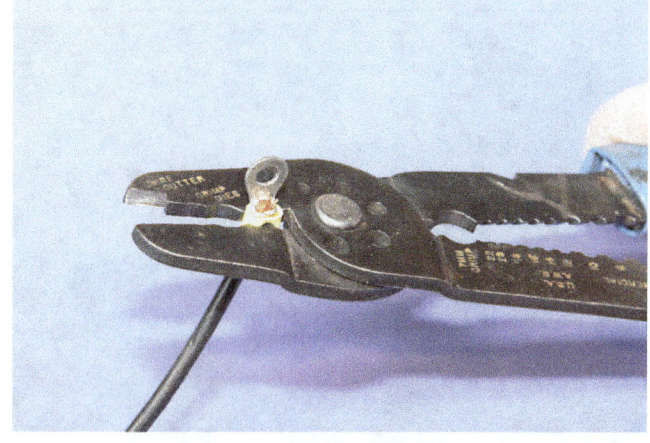

4. The regulator will come with a connector for the hot wire, which you need to crimp on prior to attaching the wire to the circuit breaker.

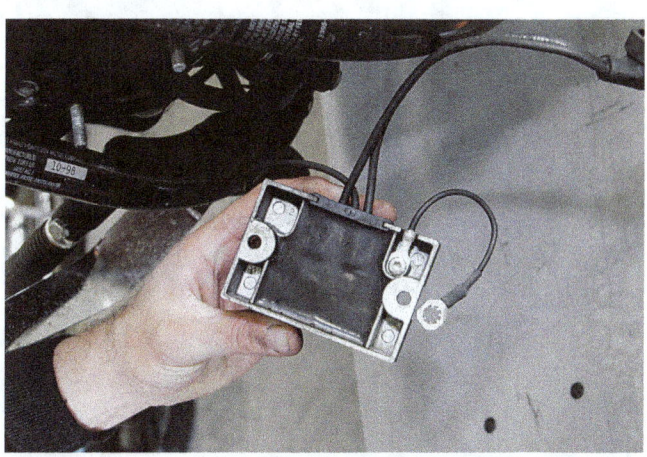

2. The rear side of the regulator. Note the separate ground cable, not all regulators have a separate ground wire, some ground though the regulator case.

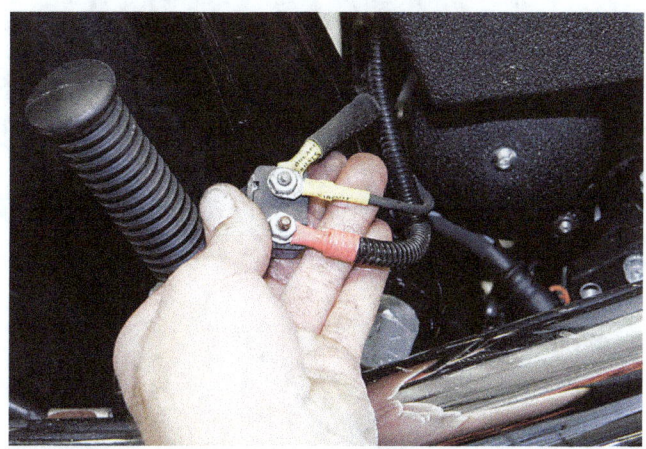

5. Here you can see the hot wire from the regulator connected to the circuit breaker, be sure to check for corrosion or loose wires when attaching the wire.

3. When you install a new regulator, it's very, very important to have a good, clean ground connection.

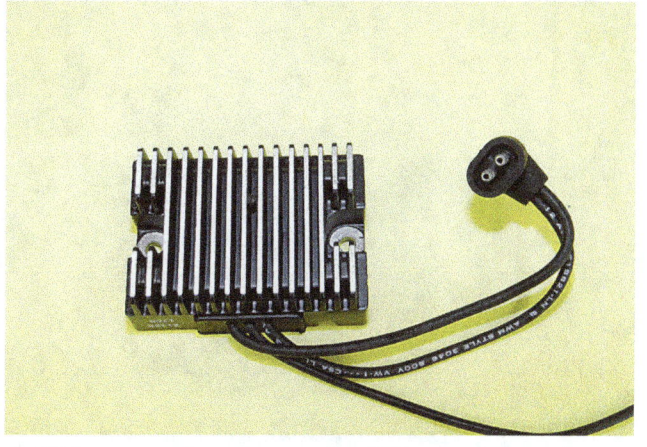

6. Voltage regulators comes in different sizes and styles. The plug goes to the stator, while the third wire is the hot wire that runs to the circuit breaker.

Charging Circuit Diagnose

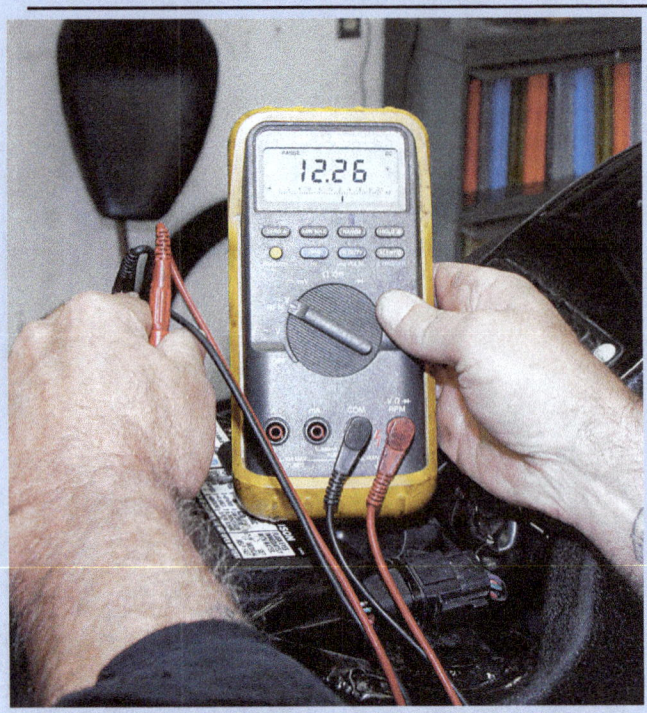

1. With the engine running and a voltmeter connected across the battery terminals, we should have 13.5 to 14.5 volts. In this case we have only battery voltage.

2. With the engine stopped, connect an ohmmeter across the stator terminals. The meter should show continuity.

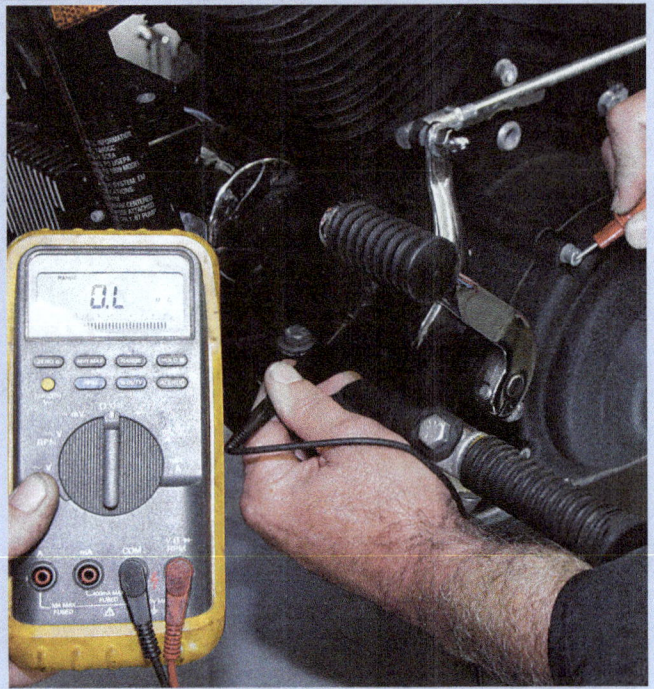

3. Using the ohmmeter again, test both the upper and lower terminals for continuity between the stator terminal and ground. If continuity exists, the stator is grounded and bad.

4. Next, run the motor at 2000 RPM, with the meter connected across the stator terminals and set to A/C voltage. There should be approx. 32 - 40 volts A/C (16 - 20/1000 RPM). If not, the stator is defective.

Charging Circuit Diagnose

Start the diagnosis of your charging circuit with a voltmeter connected across the battery terminals. With the engine running at 2000 - 2500 RPM, the voltmeter should read 13.5 to 14.5 volts.

Next, with the engine stopped, connect the ohmmeter probes across the stator wire connections as shown on the nearby photos. The ohmmeter should show continuity, (little or no resistance) between the two terminals. Now check for continuity between either terminal and ground. The meter should show no continuity (infinite resistance).

To check the raw output of the stator and rotor, connect an AC voltmeter across the two stator terminals, as shown in photo #4 on the left. Without any control by the regulator, the stator should put out AC voltage, the amount will depend on the engine's RPM.

If you have raw AC voltage, but no voltage with the regulator connected, the problem is likely the regulator. If there is no raw output, or the stator is grounded, then you're going to have to pull the primary apart and replace the stator.

With the new charging kit installed, and the engine at 2000 to 2500 RPM, we show 14.42 volts. Next we check the A/C voltage...

...with the meter connected across the stator terminals, and set to read A/C voltage, (and the engine at 2500 RPM) we now show A/C voltage output.

The Starter

How it Works

Modern Harley-Davidson starters are derived from automotive starters used on metric cars. The design uses a set of gears to take some of the load off the starter and increase the cranking speed of the motor. When you push the starter button, you send power to the starter relay. The relay in turn takes battery voltage and applies it directly to the solenoid (check the diagram below). Once energized, the solenoid does two things: it applies battery voltage from the battery cable connected to the starter, to the starter itself and it pushes the starter drive gear into mesh with the ring gear on the outside of the clutch hub. The clutch hug is connected to the engine sprocket by the primary chain. If the hub rotates, so does the engine.

Diagnosis

Many things can cause the starter not to operate. We will touch on a few basic things you should consider.

1. Make sure the battery is good, and fully charged.
2. Battery cables carry the heavy current draw, check the cables at the battery, the starter solenoid and the engine ground. Look for corrosion, loose hardware, frayed wires at lugs and any cuts in the outer covering. Tighten or replace any worn or split cables.

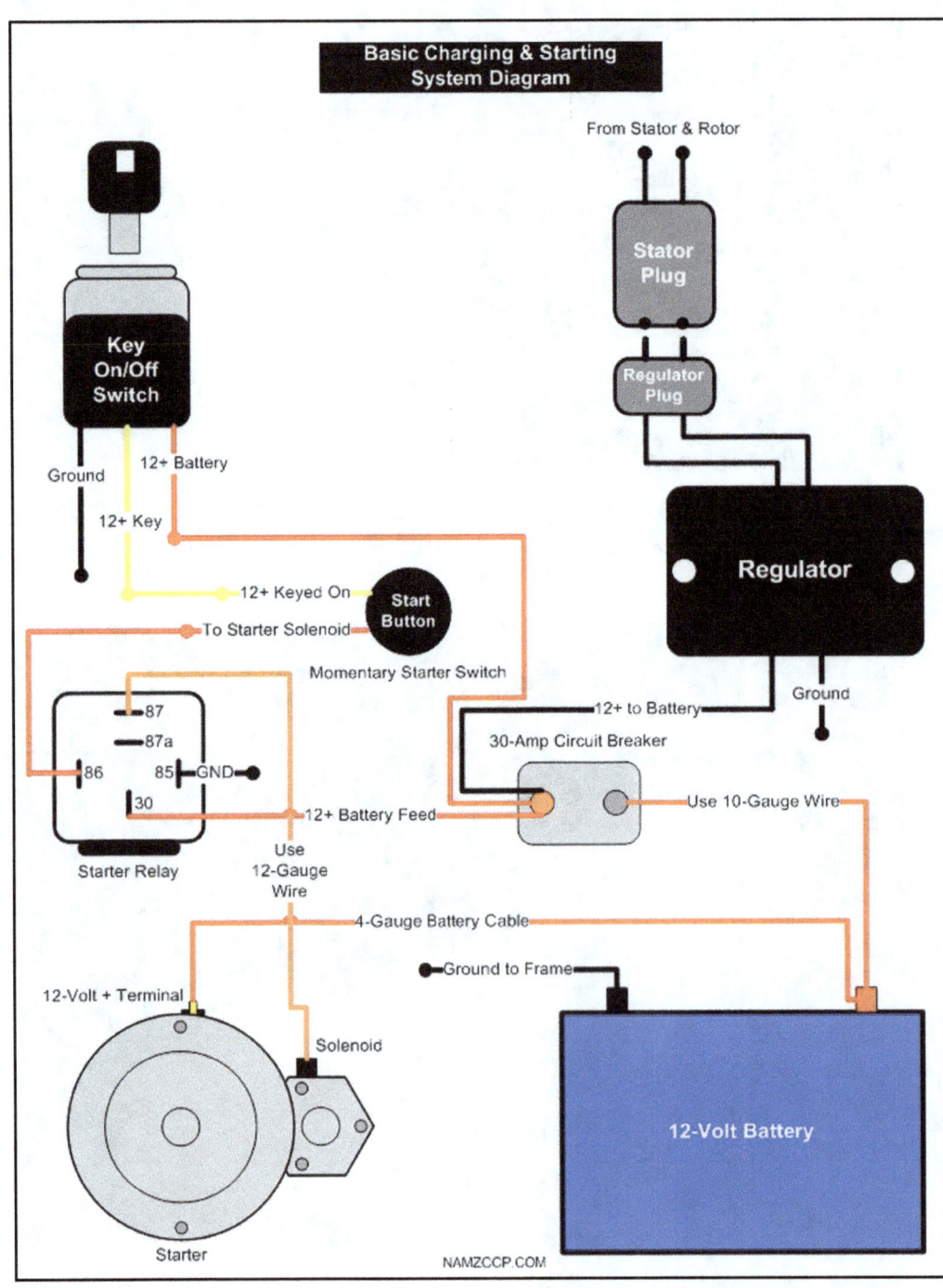

Here's a basic starter/charging circuit schematic for a late-model Harley-Davidson, and many other American V-Twins. NAMZ

3. Test the small wire on the starter solenoid using a volt meter connected to the wire and to ground. The voltmeter should read 12 volts when the starter button is engaged. If there is no power at the wire connector you must check the switch, relay, and wiring.

4. Check for voltage drop from the starter to the battery and battery to ground. Using a voltmeter check for voltage drop in the battery cables and connections.

5. If the motor turns over slowly, but the battery is good and at full charge, a current load test should be performed. (You will need an induction ammeter) Most starters in a stock motor typically will draw 160 to 180 amps. If the reading is over 200 amps the starter should be removed and checked out.

6. If the starter turns or makes a winding noise and motor doesn't spin over, the starter one-way clutch is bad, or the pinion and ring gear could be bad. Remove the outer primary cover and inspect the ring and pinion. If they are in good shape with no broken teeth or a split gear, check the one way clutch, replacement procedures can be found a little farther along in the book.

Which starter to buy?

A 1.4 KW starter is a standard unit, but if you increase the engine size or compression a larger starter may be required. You might also want to add compression releases. Harley-Davidson and many others build high quality starters, but beware of offshore units as the quality can be substandard.

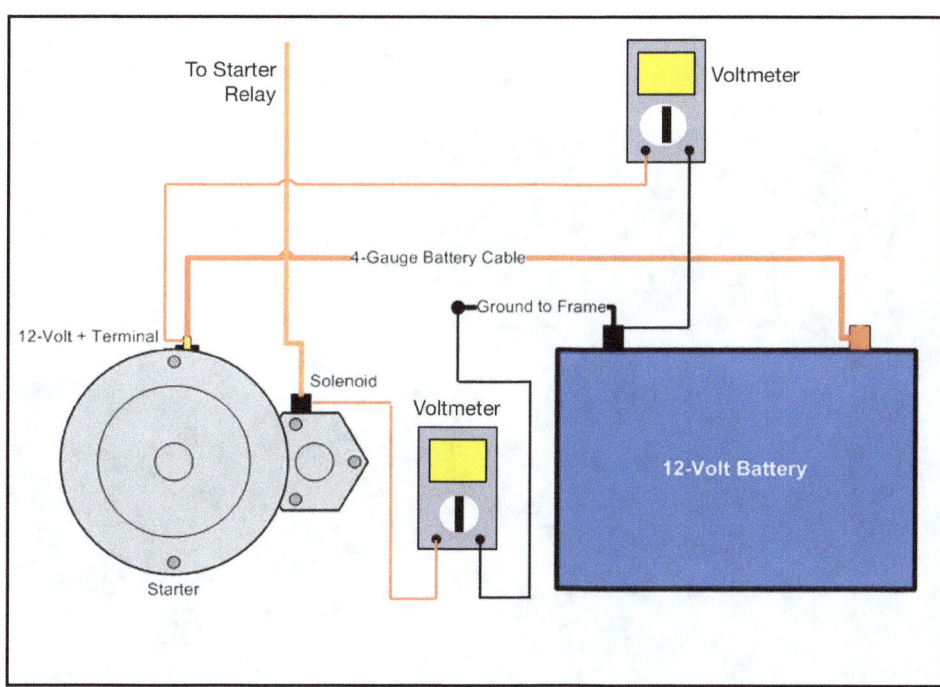

Voltmeters can be used as shown on the lower part of the image, to measure the voltage. The lower meter should read battery voltage when you hit the starter button. To measure voltage drop you connect the meter as shown in the upper part of the image. And it should be no more than one volt. NAMZ

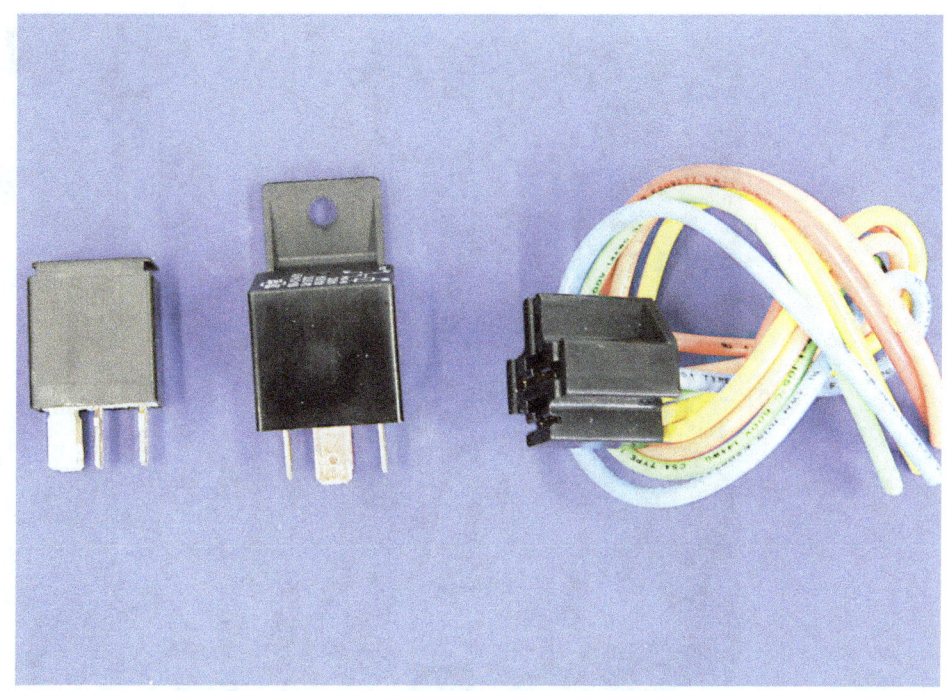

Here we have 2 starter relays and a plug assembly. As shown in the nearby schematic, nearly all V-twins use a relay in the starter circuit to take the heavy load off the starter button.

57

Starter R&R

The typical V-Twin starter bolts in from the right side as shown. Before doing anything else, disconnect the battery, negative terminal first. You can't pull the starter out until you've disassembled the jackshaft, and to do that you need to pull the primary cover off.

Next, bend back the tab that locks the jackshaft bolt (arrow) and pull off the jackshaft components. Now you can pull out the starter motor from the left side.

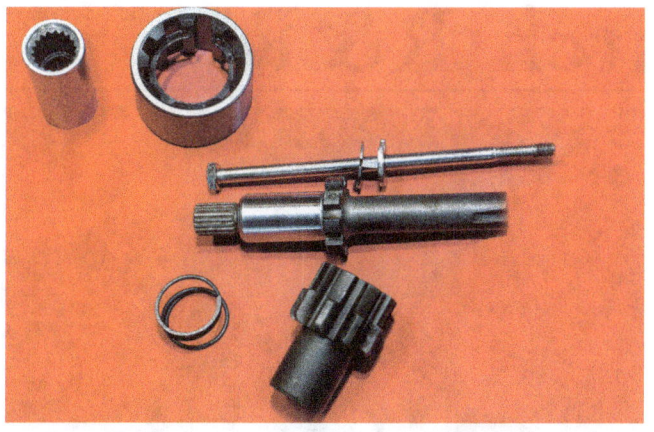

1. Reassembly: There are two couplers that are part of the starter drive (jackshaft) assembly. The smaller one has a counter bore on one end, which faces the jackshaft, not the starter.

4. Next to be installed is the drive itself...

2. After installing the starter from the other side (with the small coupler in place) the jackshaft slides in next, followed by the spring.

5. ...followed by the long jackshaft bolt, which is torqued to 7-9 ft. lbs. There is a notch in the end of the jackshaft, be sure the tab on the inside washer goes into the notch in the shaft.

3. Next up is the larger coupler, which has a shallow and deep side (there is a snap-ring inside). The shallow side intersects with the teeth on the jackshaft.

6. The tang on the end-washer is bent over and acts as a lock to prevent the long fastener from unscrewing.

Starter Clutch R&R

1. With the starter out of the bike, start by removing the rubber boot from the solenoid.

4. After bolts are removed, slide out the electric motor as a unit.

2. Next, remove the cable to the starter motor.

5. Locate the two housing screws on the output shaft side.

3. Remove bolts from the rear of the starter that go into the gear case body.

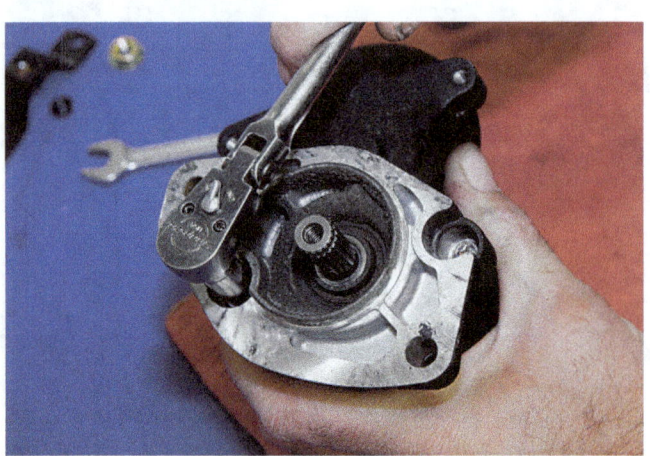

6. Remove the two screws.

1. Now the solenoid housing can be removed from the gear case.

4. Here's the idler gear and roller bearings.

2. Here's the gear case with the electric motor solenoid removed.

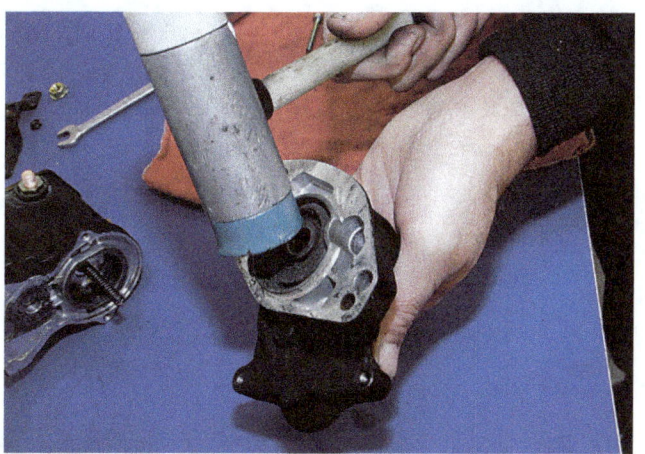

5. Tap out the stator gear, one way clutch, and O-ring. Hold it in place to seal out dirt.

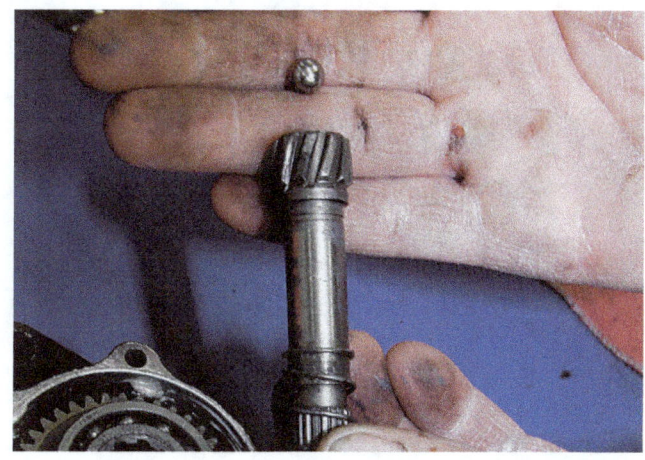

3. Remove the output shaft from the clutch. Don't drop the ball.

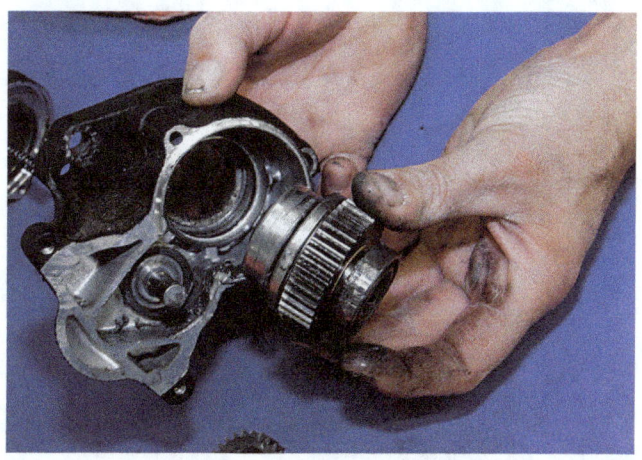

6. This is the one way starter clutch. It tends to go bad when the engine kicks back against the starter.

2. The re-assembly starts as we push the new starter clutch into the starter gear case.

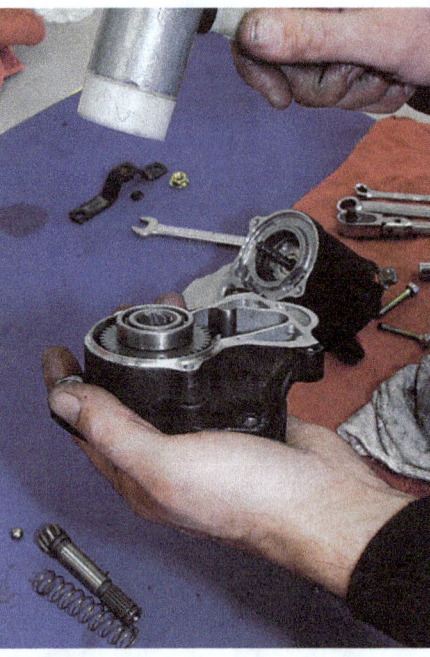

3. Next, we tap it down until it hits the bottom of the case.

4. Here you can see we've installed the idler-gear roller cage.

1. Here we have the starter gear-case components.

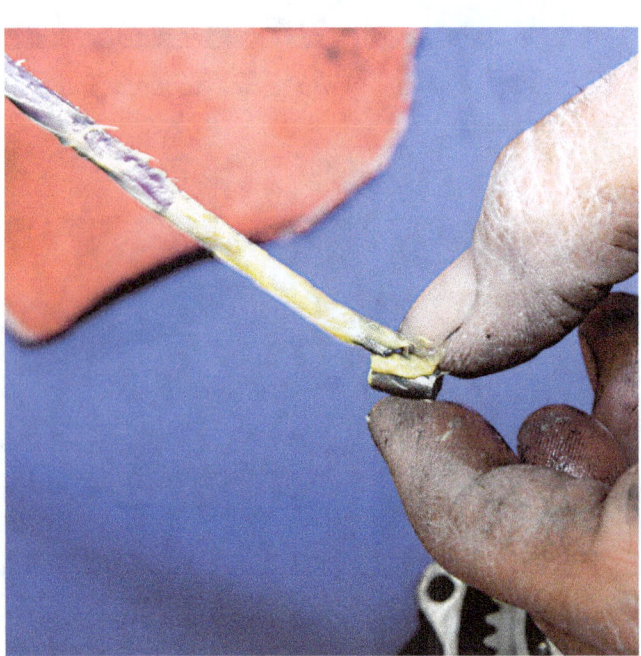

5. Lube each roller for the idler gear with white lube before installation.

1. Now, install the roller bearings into the plastic cage.

2. Next, lube the inside of the idler bearing with white lube.

4. Install the starter ball into the end of the output shaft.

3. Slide the idler gear over the idler-roller bearings.

5. More white lube, this time on the shaft of the starter clutch gear.

1. Install the gear case to the solenoid body. It should slide together easily with just spring pressure.

4. Install the long screws into the body and tighten evenly.

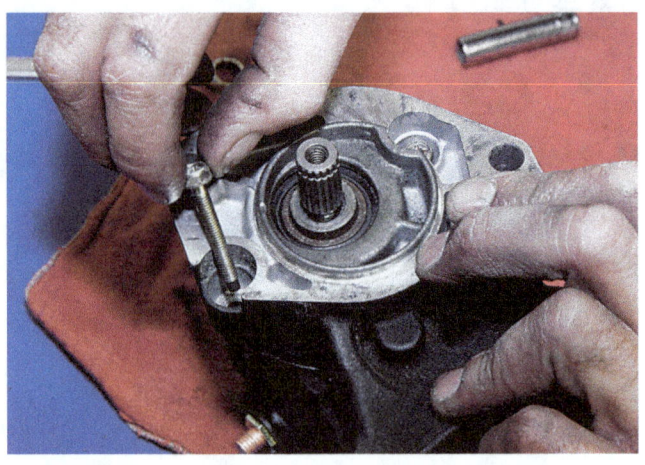

2. Before tightening, use blue Loctite on the gear case fasteners.

5. Re-install the starter cable onto the solenoid.

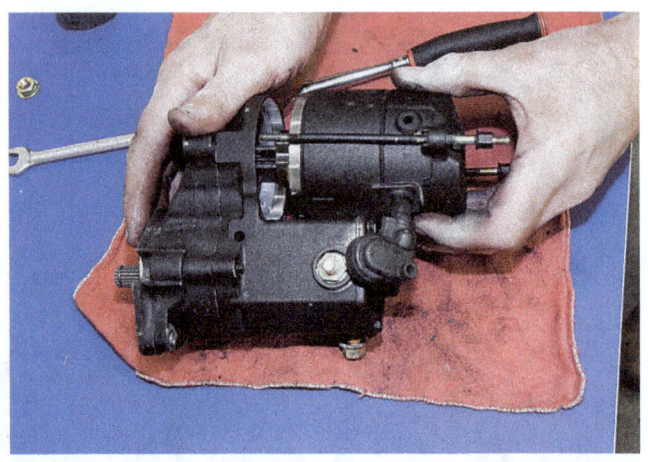

3. Now push the starter motor into gear case/solenoid unit.

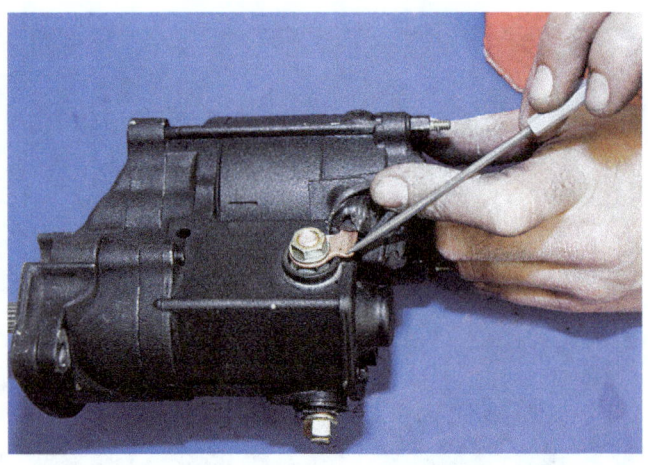

6. Be sure not to bend over the cable, you want it grounded to the case, and use caution so the stud doesn't rotate when tightening the nut.

Batteries

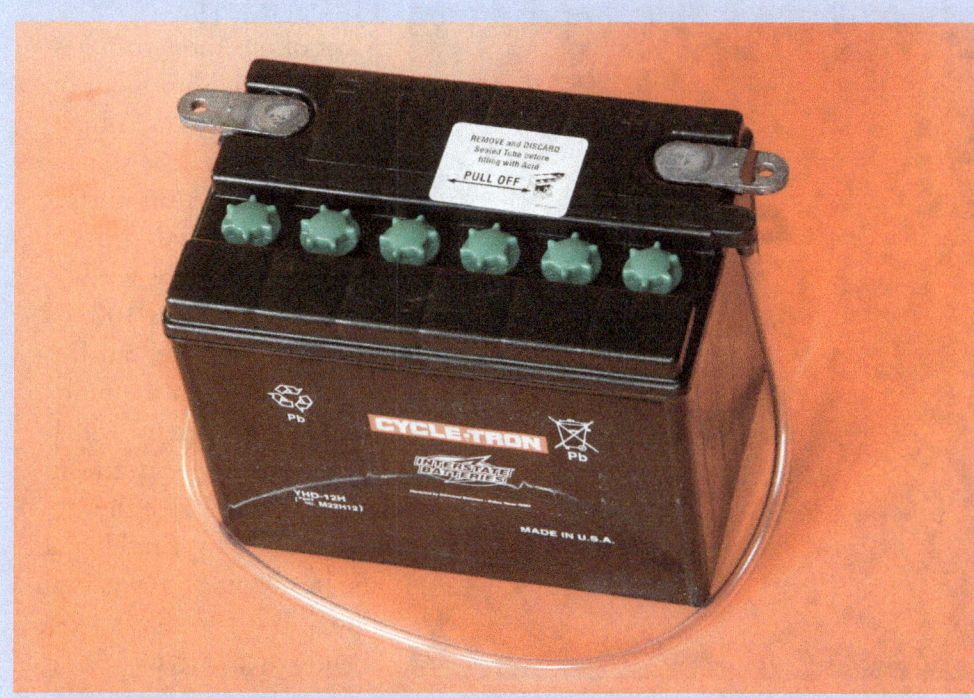

Early-style batteries like that pictured require regular checks of the electrolyte lever and the occasional addition of water.

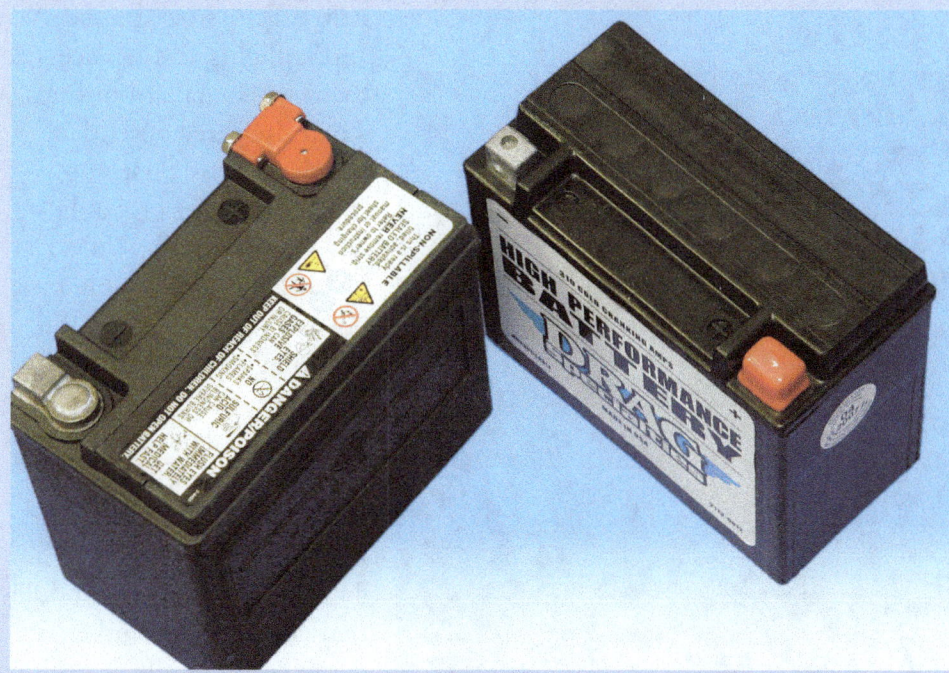

Here are two different style maintenance free batteries. Notice the difference between the positive and negative location on the two styles shown. Be sure to order a battery that fits your battery box and has the terminals in the right location for your application.

How they Work

Batteries serve two primary functions: They store energy for starting the bike, and they also stabilize the voltage of the charging system. The battery absorbs voltage spikes that occur when you rev the engine, and help to keep the voltage from going too low when you're idling at a stop light with all the lights and accessories turned on.

Once you start the engine, the battery is recharged by the charging circuit, so there's enough power available for the next start.

Maintenance

The best thing you can do for the battery is to keep it clean and charged. If the bike sits for any length of time, connect a battery-tender type charger (see the Storage Chapter). When a customers bike needs a new battery we often use a new Harley-Davidson battery.

Sealed or Not

Sealed batteries have a number of advantages. They never need to be topped off with water, they don't vent acid fumes so there are no vent tube and corrosion issues, and they generally put out more cranking power than a non-sealed battery of the same size.

Lights

Headlights come in a sealed beam (left), and those that accept a halogen bulb (right).

The halogen bulbs themselves are available in different wattages. Remember that more wattage means the bulb will draw more amperage and may pop the circuit breaker or overheat the wiring at the back of the bulb.

HEADLIGHTS

Most of our modern bikes run a halogen headlight bulb with two filaments, a high and low beam. The standard bulb is rated 55/60 watts, for high and low beam. High output bulbs with wattages as high as 100 watts are available, but the extra watts mean the bulb draws more current, which means you might overheat the wiring or cause the circuit breaker to trip. Upgrade the headlight bulb with caution.

TURN SIGNALS/ TAILLIGHTS

The first thing a lot of owners do with a new bike is strip off the stock blinkers and taillights and replace them with smaller housings. There are three potential problems here. First, the smaller housing probably has a smaller bulb. Unless it's an LED, it probably puts out less light, meaning the cars are going to have trouble seeing the light when you signal a left turn. Second, the new lights may not be DOT approved, and might get you a ticket. Third, the flasher or module that controls the blinkers is designed to handle a specific amount of current. If you reduce that amount you may have to add a load equalizer so the signals operate correctly.

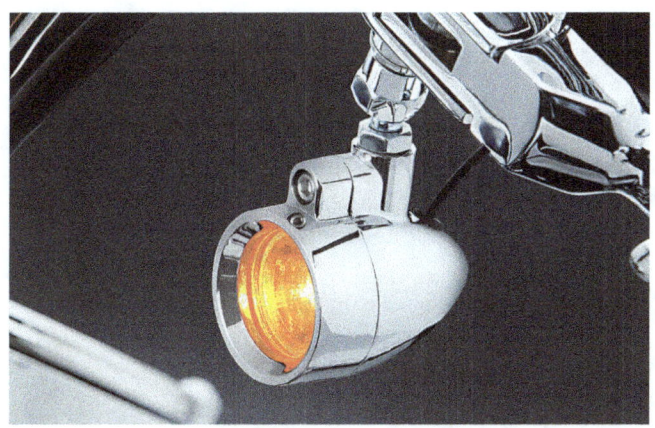

A wide variety of aftermarket lights are available to replace the large, stock lights that come on new bikes. Buy lights bright enough so that other bikes and cars can see the light. Kuryakyn

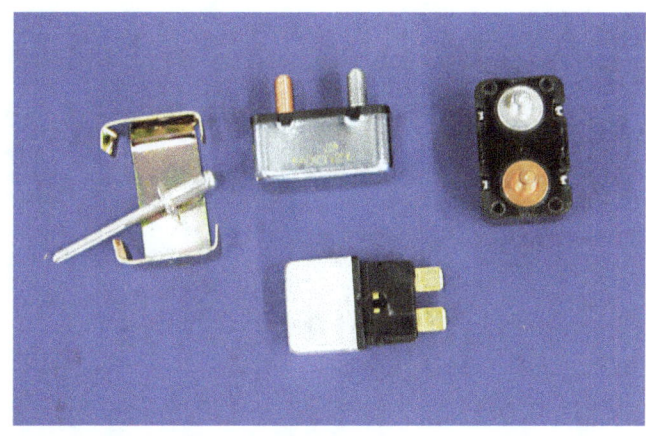

Circuit breakers typically come in two physical sizes and are rated for either 15 or 30 amps.

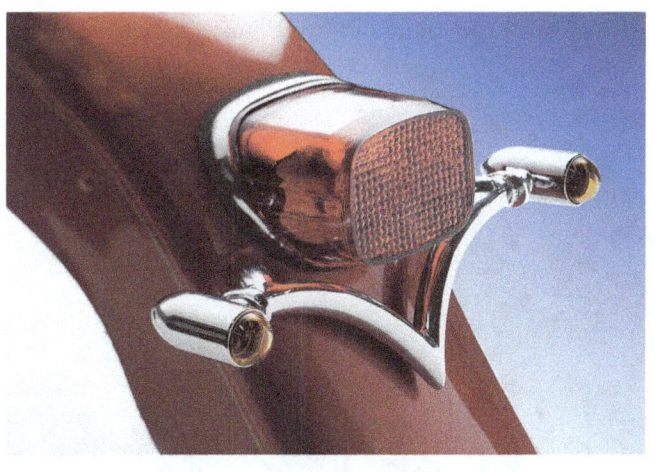

There are a variety of ways to replace the bulky light bar found on many stock bikes without losing the turn signals altogether. CCI

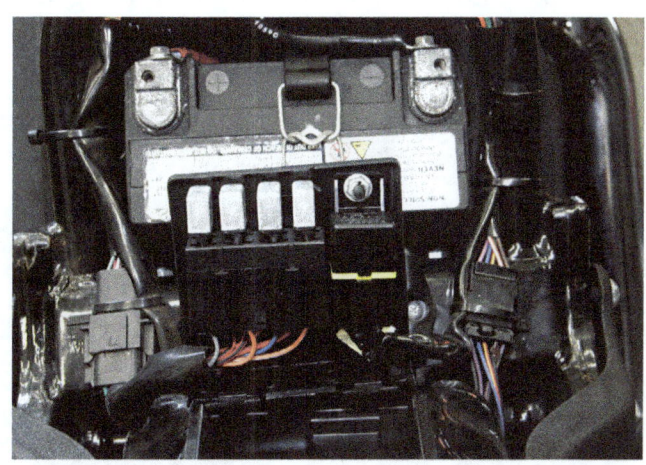

Softail fuse panels are located under the seat, set into the rear fender.

When aftermarket lights are used in place of factory units, you will likely have to also add a load equalizer for correct turn signal operation.

On Dressers the fuse panel is mounted under the left side-cover.

Chapter Six

Tires, Wheels, Bearings

Keep it Rolling Free

Whether you're doing something simple like swapping out a tire, or installing a set of wheel bearings, you have to be careful with each step. These parts hold up the bike, they keep you going down the road.

Always take the time to do the job carefully. Use Loctite on the threads of the fasteners, as shown here and in your service manual. Follow the torque recommendations for axle nuts and any other nuts and bolts. Though we've recorded the

The tires, wheels and bearings are among the most important parts of your motorcycle. Safe riding means regular inspection and maintenance of all these parts.

Softail Rear Wheel R&R

torque specifications for the jobs seen here, be sure to check the specs for your year and model.

We've tried to cover all the basics: how to take the wheel on and off the front and rear of different model bikes, how to get the tire off the wheel without a tire machine, and how to replace and service wheel bearings whether they're the old-style tapered bearings, or the more modern sealed wheel bearings.

The projects might seem to overlap, but we think it's better to show too many bikes than not enough. This way we're more likely to include a bike that's the same as the one you ride. The wheel R&R sequences include both a late model Bagger with eccentrics for the belt adjustment, and a Softail with the threaded adjustment on either side. The double threaded adjusters require more work, and care, when it comes time to adjust the belt tension and the position of the rear wheel in the swingarm.

Don't skimp when you repair the wheels and tires on the bike. If the tires look a little sketchy, buy new ones. If the bearings feel a little rough, install a new pair. After all, the only thing holding you up off the ground is two tires, each one supported by a wheel and a set of bearings.

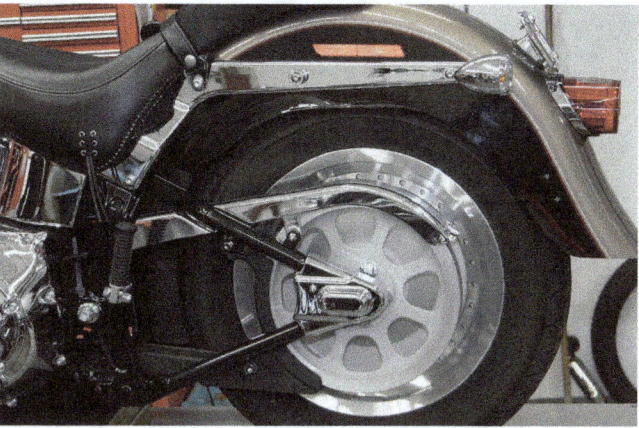

1. The problem: your tire is going flat after 10 minutes. This is a typical Softail rear wheel and tire.

2. Remove axel cover if so equipped. The cover is an add-on and not from the Motor Factory.

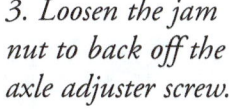

3. Loosen the jam nut to back off the axle adjuster screw.

69

1. Remove the axle cover mounting plate.

4. Loosen and remove the axel nut and adjuster washer.

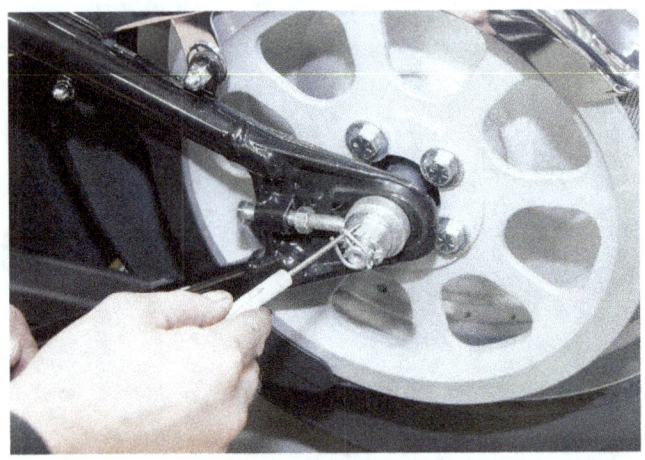

2. Remove the axle nut locking clip or cotter pin.

5. Slide the axle out, on some models the exhaust must be removed first.

3. Remove the belt guard. This is not necessary on all models, but if it makes the removal easier - go ahead and take it off.

6. Be careful with the wheel spacers. Take note of the placement. They must go back in where they came out.

1. Slide the rear caliper out of the way to access the wheel.

4. Slide the caliper back into place. Note, the caliper is effectively one of the wheel spacers.

2. Raise the cycle to make tire removal easier, the wheel assembly slides out with a tilting motion.

5. There is a spacer on each side. Again, make sure they go back in to the right place.

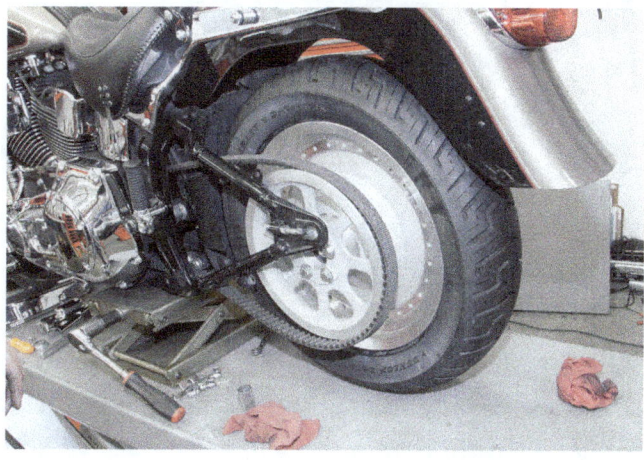

3. After the tire repair, reinstall the wheel under the cycle (see the tire R&R/repairs).

6. Use anti-seize compound on the axle and bearings so they don't rust in place and make the next disassembly difficult.

1. Lower the cycle to line everything up and make the axle installation easier.

4. The distance is measured from the center of the swingarm pivot bolt to the center of the axle. This distance must be the same on both sides.

2. Here the axle shaft is installed through the left side wheel and spacer.

5. With the cycle on the ground, rotate the tire to the tightest point in the belt. Then adjust the belt tension to 5/16 to 3/8 inch of up and down movement.

3. Install the adjuster shim and nut. Don't over tighten the axle nut until the adjustment is finished. The tool shown here is used to measure the position of the axle and get it even from side to side.

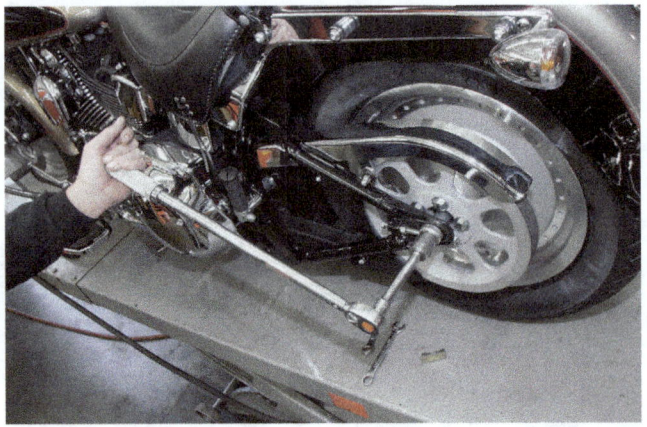

6. Once the belt is adjusted, torque the rear axle nut to 65 ft. lbs. Re-install the lock pin or cotter clip.

Bagger Rear Wheel R&R

1. Remove the axle-nut locking clip.

2. Using a 36mm socket, loosen the axle nut.

3. Note the taper on the outside of the axle nut.

4. The cam is used to set the belt tension. It has a flat spot on the axle and only goes on one way. Most Baggers need to have the muffler removed to slide the axle out.

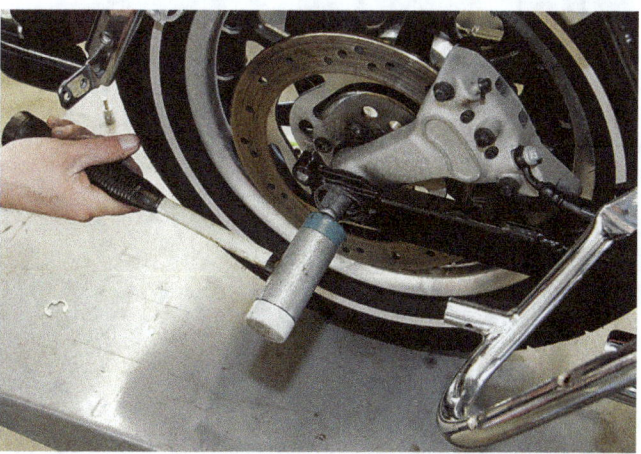

5. Tap out the axle. Use a soft hammer so as not to damage the axle.

1. Slide out the axle. Note: make sure the muffler is out of the way.

4. Remove the inner rear wheel spacer. Note the way the spacer comes out, it only goes in one way.

2. Walk the drive belt over the belt pulley as shown.

5. Remove the small spacer sandwiched between the wheel bearing and caliper.

3. Take the belt off of the pulley and pull it to the side.

6. Lift the cycle (note the jack) until the caliper becomes loose or free.

1. Get the caliper up and out of the way, this gives you room to remove the wheel assembly.

2. With a tilting motion, remove the wheel assembly.

3. This is a part of this job, but it is worth mentioning: Spin the wheel bearing with your finger. Feel for any flat spots, or looseness.

4. Reinstallation, get the wheel positioned under the swingarm.

5. Slowly lower the cycle until the wheel is almost at fender height.

1. Before reinstalling the caliper, look to see that the rubber bumper is in place under the brake stay.

4. Install the large spacer on the belt-pulley side.

2. With the caliper in position, lower the bike to align the swingarm and the center of the wheel.

5. Brush a liberal amount of anti-seize on the axle before installation.

3. Install the small spacer under the caliper. Note that the caliper carrier also acts as a spacer.

6. After the cycle is lowered to the correct height, slide the axle through swing arm, spacers and wheel.

1. On the right side, align the caliper and spacers so the axle slides through.

4. ...rotate the tire and wheel until you find the tightest spot in the belt. Now adjust the wheel position to obtain 5/16 to 3/8 inch of up and down play.

2. Position adjusting cam onto the axle and screw the nut on the axle until finger tight.

5. Torque the axle nut to 105 ft. lbs. You must hold the opposite side of the axle at the same time so it does not rotate.

3. Adjust the belt tension by turning the axle with a socket wrench...

6. Snap the axle safety E-clip into the slot and reinstall the exhaust and accessories.

Sealed Bearing Replacement

1. The front wheel of a FLHT in the clamp, ready for service.

4. With a wrench on the flats, turn the large outside nut to pull the bearing (removing the rotor made it easier to get at the flats on the threaded shaft).

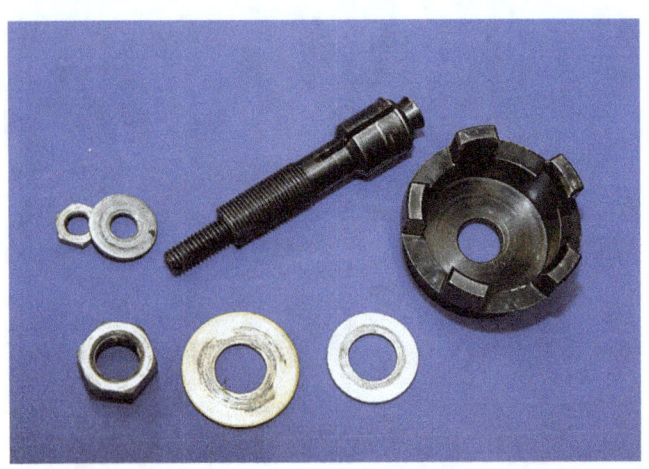

2. A sealed wheel bearing removal tool by JIMS.

5. The removed wheel bearing, still on the removal tool.

3. The bearing removal tool in place on the wheel. Note the flats on the outer, threaded, shaft.

6. Prior to installing the bearings, lubricate the outside bearing surface with oil.

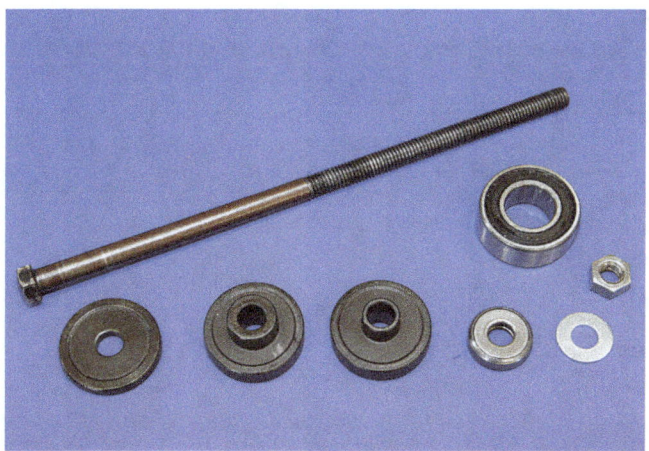

1. The bearing installation tool kit by JIMS.

2. The installer tool comes in from the other side. Put the new bearing on the shaft, as shown, with the heavy washer (aka pressure plate) and nut.

4. ...this will pull the wheel bearing into place, use oil on the tool threads and any place where there is metal to metal contact.

3. Tighten the nut down onto the pressure plate...

5. The bearing installed in the hub. The new bearing should go in without binding.

79

Tapered Wheel Bearing Service

1. To start, remove the grease seals with a puller or a large, flat screwdriver.

4. Here are the spacer shims. These are used to set the end play, don't lose them.

2. Once the seal is out of the way...

5. Next is the wheel center-spacer. These also come in assorted dimensions.

3. ...you can pop the bearing out of the hub. Carefully inspect the bearing and race for metal chips, rust or pits. Be sure to clean all the old grease out of the hub.

6. Shown are wheel bearings, spacer and shims. Shims come in different thicknesses and are used to adjust the bearing end play. Thicker shims provide more end play, thinner will create less end play.

Pack the Bearings

When you pack the bearings you can either do it by hand, (as shown in the Fork and Neck chapter) or you can do it as seen here - with a packer that's available from most parts stores for about twenty dollars.

No matter whether you pack the bearings by hand or with a mechanical device, the important thing is to actually force the grease up between the rollers, you can't just coat the outside of the bearing with grease.

The grease needs to be rated for wheel bearing use. At Shadley Bros., we like to use waterproof wheel bearing grease.

Before packing and installing the bearings, be sure to inspect both the rollers and the bearing race. A bad bearing or race means replacing both components, the bearing and the matching race. If the bearing races are OK, coat them with a coating of grease before you install the tapered bearing.

Though the later model Harley-Davidsons, and most of the new aftermarket wheels, use sealed bearings, there are still plenty of older bikes and aftermarket wheels around that use the tapered bearings.

1. This the wheel bearing packer found in many shops.

3. Install the top, and compress the packer to force grease through the bearing.

2. Install the bearing in the packer, tapered end down.

4. Presto, a packed wheel bearing. If you look closely, you can see that the grease has been forced up between each of the rollers.

Set Wheel Bearing End-Play

1. This is our bearing end-play and run-out stand. To start, slide a bearing and a spacer onto the fixture...

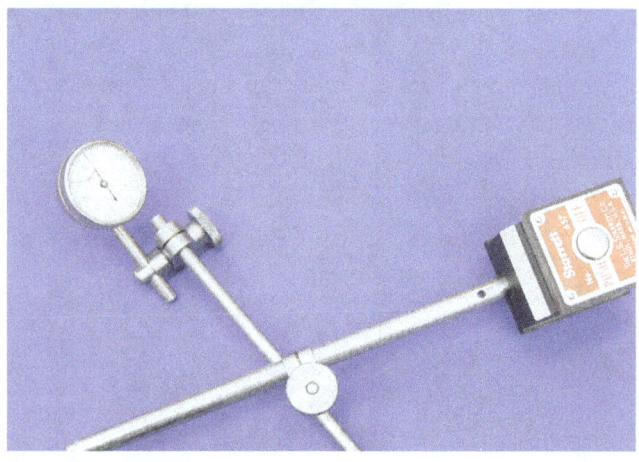

4. We use a dial indicator with a magnetic stand to measure end-play.

2. ...next, slide the wheel onto the stand, install the outer bearing, the outer spacer and lock nut.

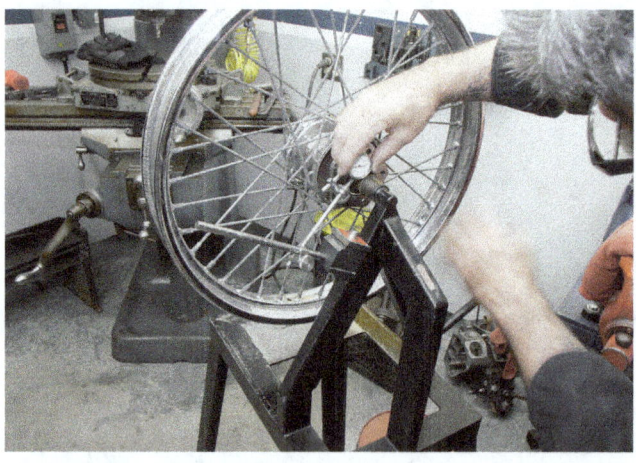

5. Mount the stand so the dial indicator reads off the flat flange of the hub.

3. The wheel must rotate freely, look for wheel run out - both up and down, and side to side.

6. Move the wheel back and forth to check the total amount of end-play. Use thicker or thinner shims to adjust the end play to the factory specs.

Front Wheel R&R

1. Before starting, place a jack under the chassis and lift the weight from the front wheel.

2. Remove the caliper mounting screws, these are 10mm, 12 point.

4. Remove the nut and washer from the axle.

3. Axle nuts are 15/16 inch on late model 2008, and 3/4 inch on early models 2007 and older.

5. Remove the two strap nuts and washers.

1. Tap the axle out from the wheel using a soft mallet.

4. Lift the front of the bike up so the tire clears the fender and then remove the wheel from the bike.

2. Pull the axle completely out from the fork assembly.

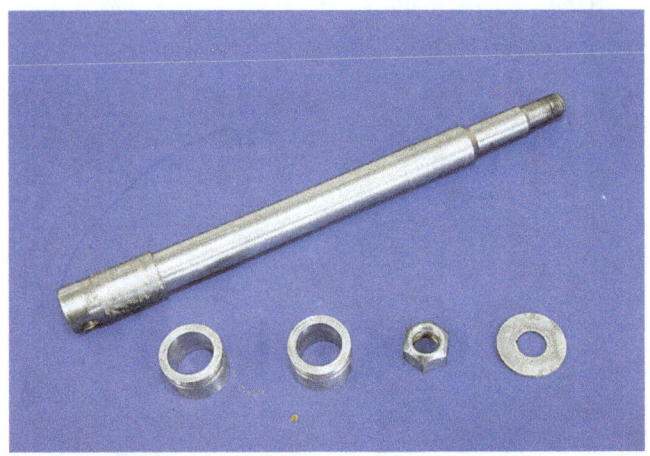

5. Late model axle spacers and hardware. The late model Baggers use a hollow axle.

3. As always, the spacer can be a different size on each side. Pay attention to which spacer is on which side of the axle.

6. Clean the axle and apply anti-seize prior to reassembly.

1. Lower the bike so the axle will slide through the lower leg into the wheel. Slide the axle through the leg and the spacer, into the wheel.

4. Tighten the axle strap nuts to 132 to 180 in. lbs.

2. Push the axle through the left side lower leg (aka the slider) and tighten axle nut until seated.

5. Install the caliper over the rotors. Torque the caliper mounting bolts to 28 - 30 ft. lbs.

3. Torque axle nut: 15/16 inch nut (2008 and up) to 65 ft. lbs. Models with 3/4 inch nut (2007 and earlier) to 50 - 55 ft. lbs.

6. The front wheel reinstalled. Be sure to seat the brake pads by pumping the brake lever **before** you take the first ride.

Tire R&R

1. Check for leaks with a soapy water solution. The bubbles indicate a rim leak.

4. Before removing the tire, spray the rim and tire with tire lube. Use two tire irons to lift the tire over the rim.

2. First, push the tire from the rim bead. Note the chalk line, you want to reinstall the tire in the same position on the rim.

5. With the tire irons, lift the tire over the rim, always use rim guards to protect the rim.

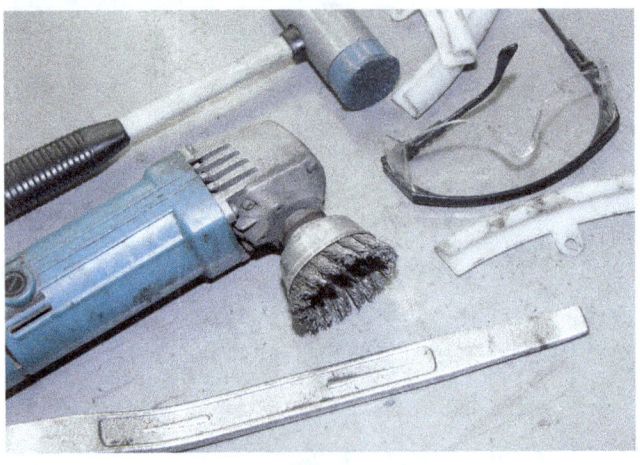

3. These are the assorted tire repair tools and rim guards we use in the shop.

6. Now pull the tire over the rim completely.

Tire R&R

1. Use the guard on the rim again, as you work the other tire bead over the rim.

4. Keep the tire bead in the center of the rim, as that is the narrowest part of the rim and will make it easier to get the bead over the edge of the rim.

2. Buff the inside of the rim, clean all rubber and oxidation from the sealing surface.

5. Getting the second bead over the rim is a matter of working slowly around the edge of the tire, note the rim guards.

3. With lube on the tire, start the reinstallation by pushing one side over the rim lip.

6. Once you have the tire installed on the rim be sure to align the chalk mark with the valve stem, inflate the tire, and check for leaks.

Chapter Seven

Forks & Neck

Overhaul the Forks & Pack the Neck Bearings

If a fork starts to weep oil at the seal or leak fluid it should be dismantled and inspected. Check for worn bushings, and the condition of the slider and fork tube. Be sure to replace any worn parts. If none are found, replace the seal and refill the fork assembly with the proper amount of fork oil. You can check your owner's manual for the correct amount of oil, and the recommended viscosity, needed for your particular model.

Fork oils come in different viscosities, from a

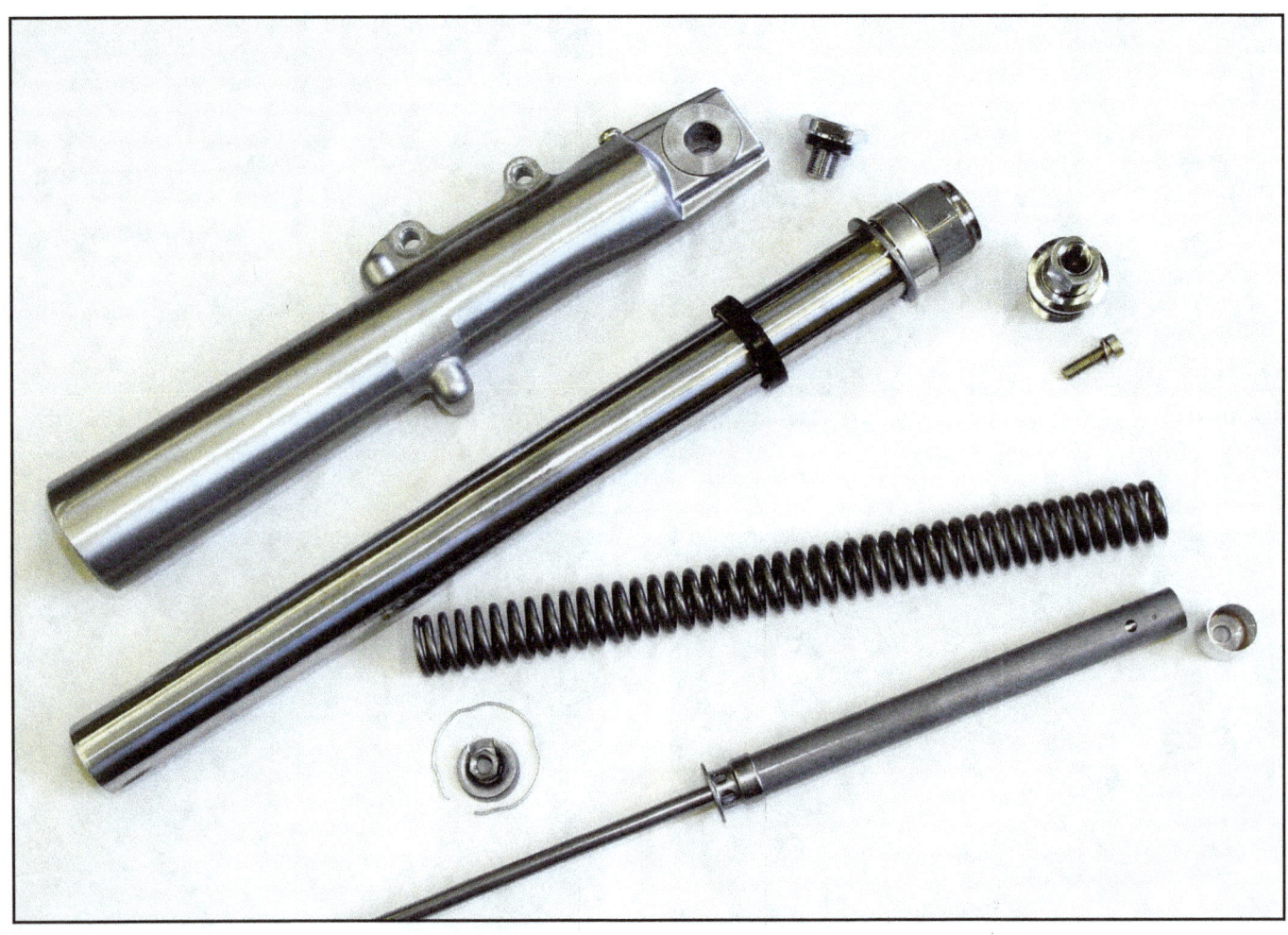

A 41mm lower slider assembly from a full Dresser, dismantled, cleaned and ready to assemble. Some of the new, more sophisticated forks have a "cartridge" damper unit, seen at the bottom.

light 5w oil to a heavier 20w fluid. The weight does have a noticeable effect on the damping of the front suspension. A lightweight solo rider might like a lightweight oil, while a heavier rider who often rides double often prefers a 15 or 20w oil in the forks.

Most fork-tube assemblies have a small drain plug, so you can drain the fork without a complete disassembly. We like to see people change the oil every 10,000 miles or 24 months.

You can do more than just change the viscosity of the oil, in order to "tune" the fork to your own riding style. The other thing you can do is change the springs in the fork. Fork springs come in various lengths and types. Some are progressive or variable, like some of the shock absorber springs that are wound more tightly on one end. This way, when you hit a small bump that requires only a little fork compression, the fork is basically pretty soft. On a bigger bump the fork goes progressively from soft to firm as the amount of compression increases.

Springs also come with different ratings. Like shock springs, they're rated according to how much weight it takes to create a certain amount of compression.

When you buy fork springs you have to decide whether or not you want to stay with the stock ride height, and then you need to decide on the right rating.

Here's a typical Road King headlight nacelle. First remove lower screw from outside headlamp ring. Lift out and up.

Remove Phillips screws from outside of headlamp mounting housing.

To release the wire plug squeeze the two release tabs and wiggle the plug off gently.

The are many wires to keep track of. Make a diagram or take a photo to aid with reassembly. Unplug the turn signal wiring harness. Lift the lock tab as shown to release.

1. Unplug the spot lamp connection.

3. Lift up the nacelle center trim and it will come free from the handlebar clamp cover.

2. Remove the upper and lower light bar screws.

4. Gently pry up the steering head lock finish bezel. It is held in place by small clips.

5. Remove Phillips screws from handlebar clamp cover.

91

1. Remove the front screw from top cover.

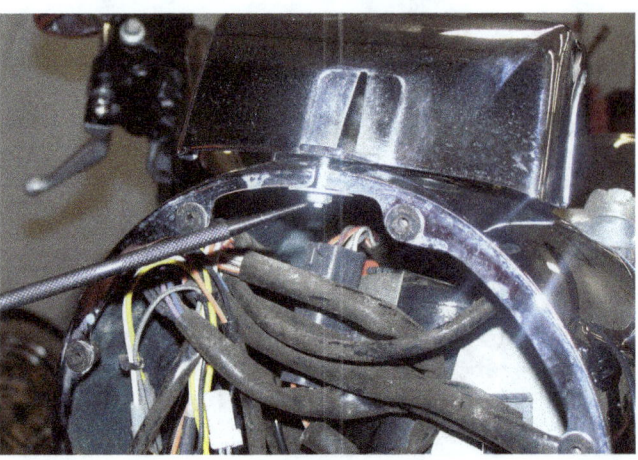

2. Remove the small nut located inside the nacelle as shown.

3. Lift up and out, then slide downward away from the forks

4. Unplug the driving light plug.

5. Here you can see the nacelle at this stage of the disassembly.

1. After taking off the left side of the nacelle, remove the right nacelle half.

2. Here's a clear look at the wiring under the nacelle.

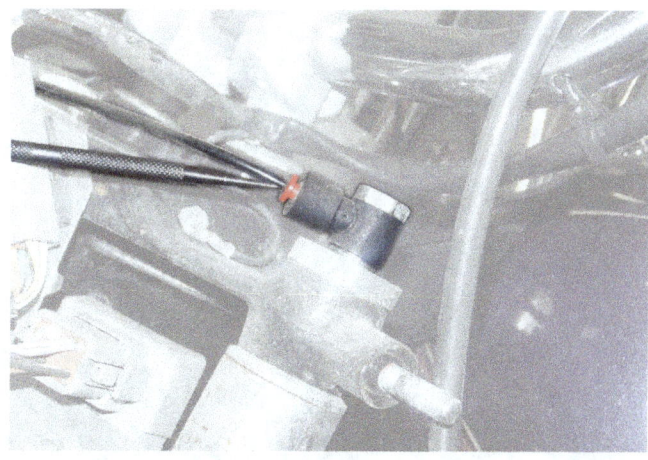

3. Release air, if so equipped, from air valve. Push in the outside of red lock collar...

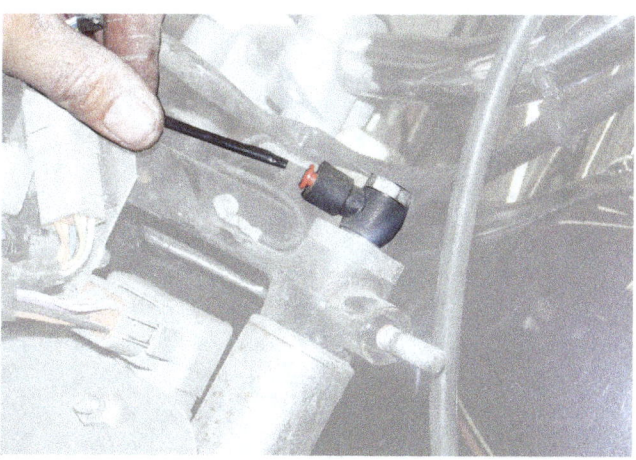

4. ...and pull out the air line.

5. Remove the through bolt on top of the fork bolt.

6. Remove the fork bolt from the top of triple clamps on both sides.

1. Only remove the bolt half way to prevent fork assembly from falling to the ground.

2. Here's the fork bolt being removed.

4. If the fork tube is jammed or rusted with top bolt, back it out two full turns and tap with block of wood. Continue one turn at a time until bolt is almost removed.

3. Remove the lower triple tree fork clamp bolts.

5. Spray lubrication on the tube for easy removal of the fork stop bushing.

1. Here's the fork tube half way out of the top clamp.

2. If the tube will not slide out it may be necessary to spread open the lower triple tree slot with a thin chisel.

3. Place the tube in a vice. We use brass jaws in our vice to minimize damage to the components.

4. Remove the lower fork slider bolt, it is a 6mm Allen screw.

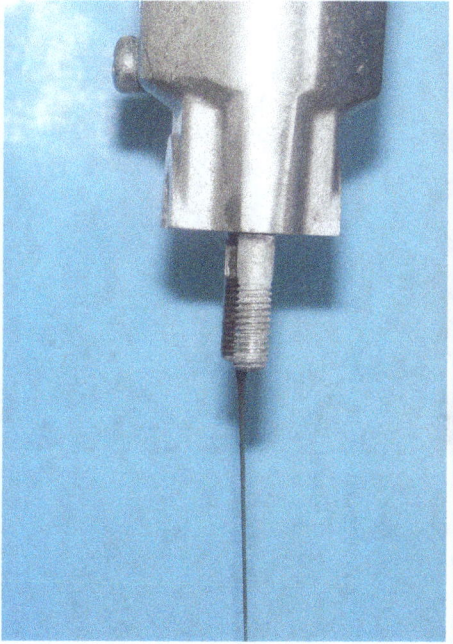
5. Drain fluid into a drain pan and dispose of properly.

6. Locate the upper seal-retaining clip.

1. Use a small screwdriver to remove the upper fork-seal retaining clip.

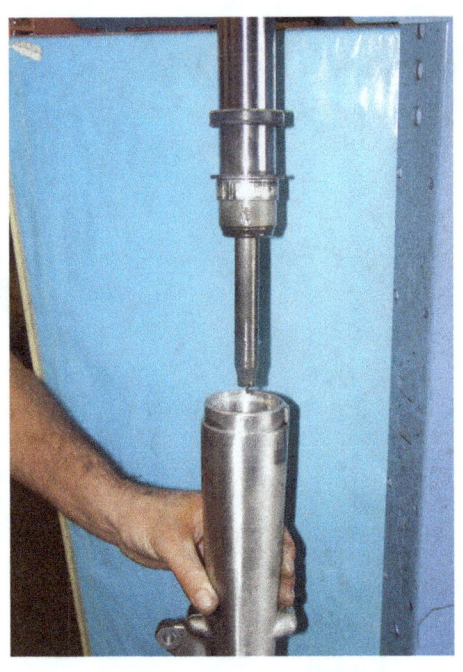

2. Separate the lower slider from the fork tube by sliding the two apart in a jerking stroke until the seal pops out of the lower leg.

3. Remove the upper fork tube plug.

4. Remove the two slider bushings from fork tube. Split lower bushing open to slide off the two with a small screwdriver as shown.

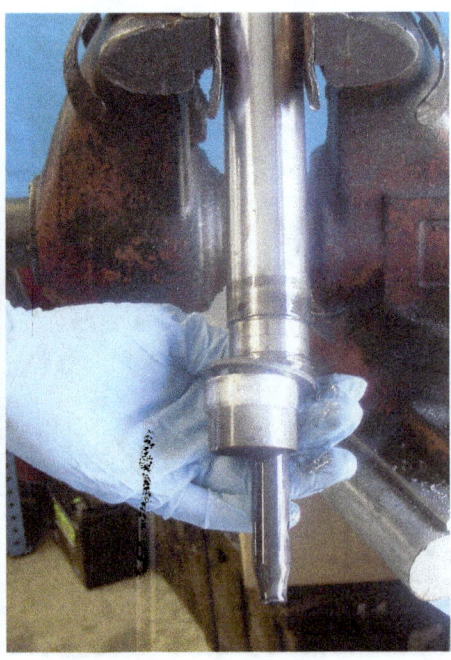

5. The upper bushing will slide off with the upper seal spacer.

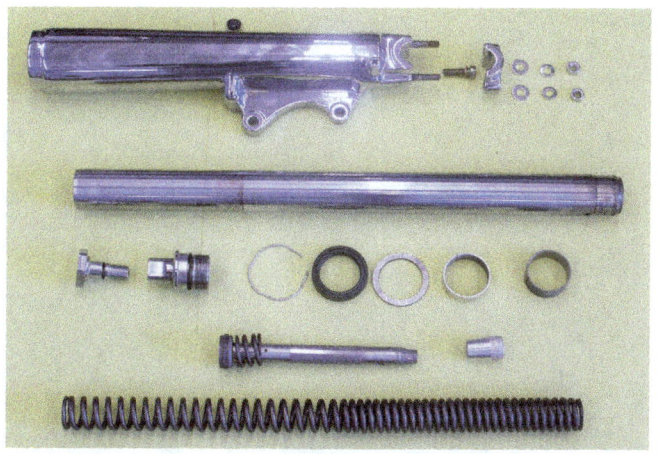

1. Here's the fork assembly, cleaned and ready for reassembly.

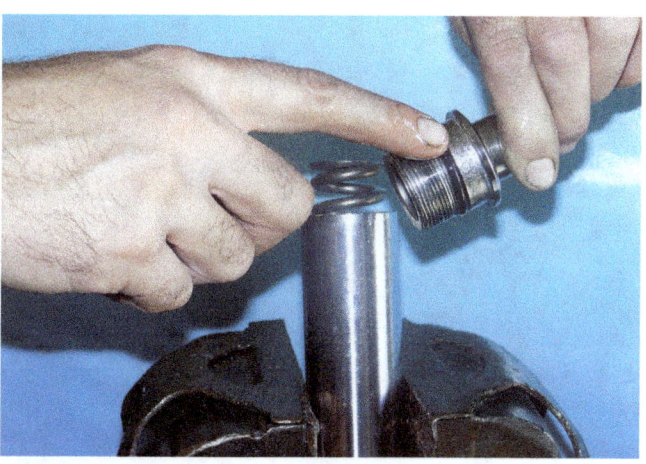

3. Next, install the fork spring, then replace the upper fork tube O-ring, and lube with fork oil.

2. Here is the damper tube removed from the fork tube. After checking for wear on upper ring, start the reassembly by dropping the damper tube into the fork tube.

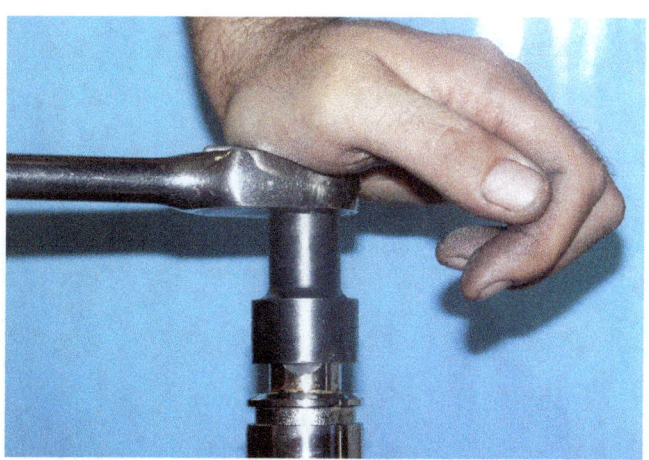

4. Install the upper plug into fork tube and tighten. Push downward to overcome the spring tension.

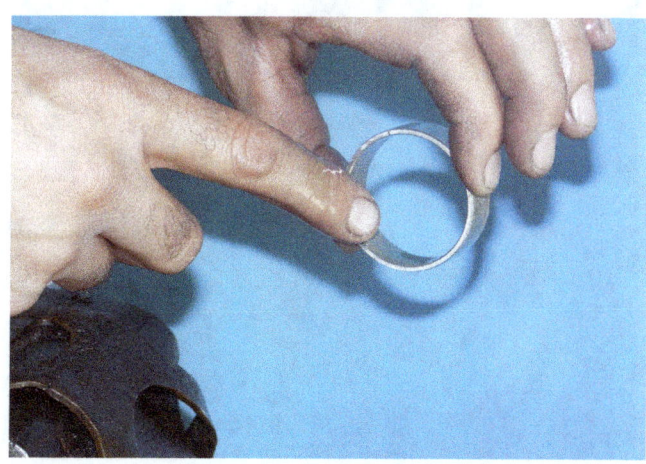

5. Inspect the fork bushing for wear, and lube it prior to assembly.

1. The fork seal must be installed correctly, there is a top and a bottom. The lip faces down, if installed incorrectly it will leak.

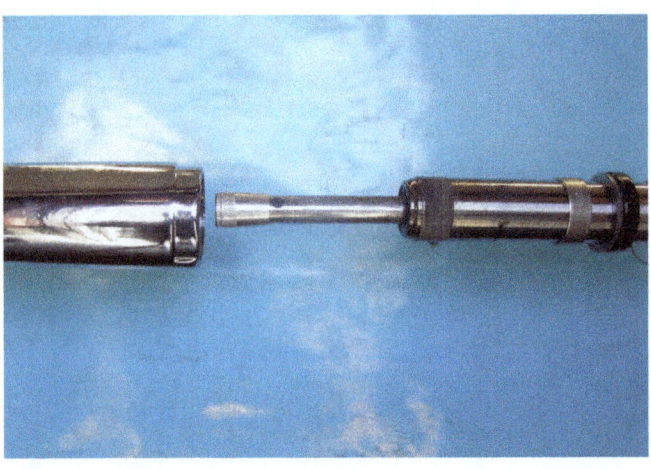

3. The upper fork tube assembly and bushing being inserted into the lower fork leg.

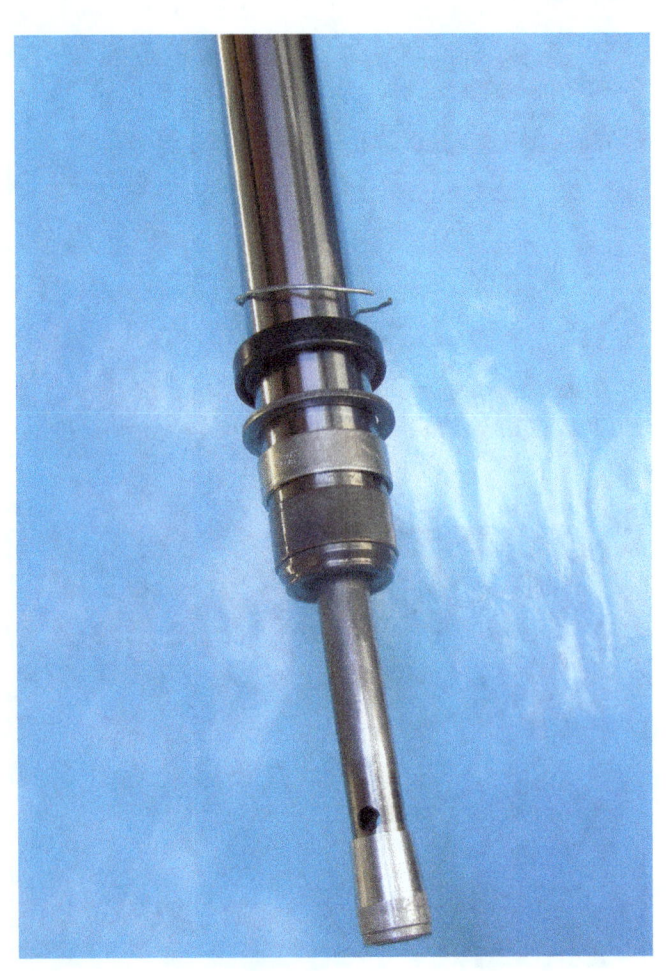

2. Here is the fork tube with damper tube and lower stop prior to being placed into the slider or lower leg.

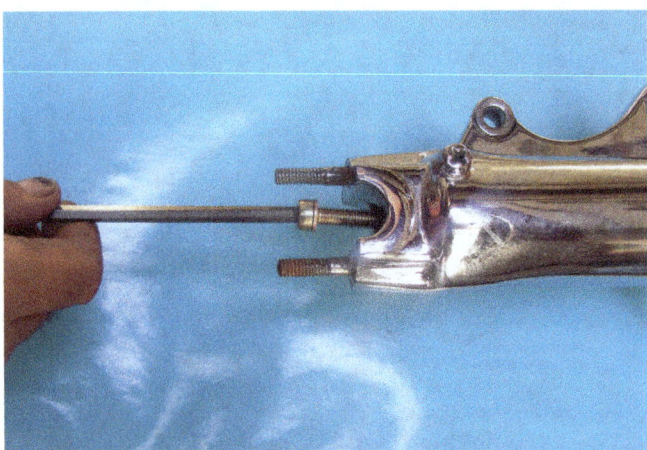

4. Screw the retaining bolt into the damper tube assembly by hand until it bottoms out.

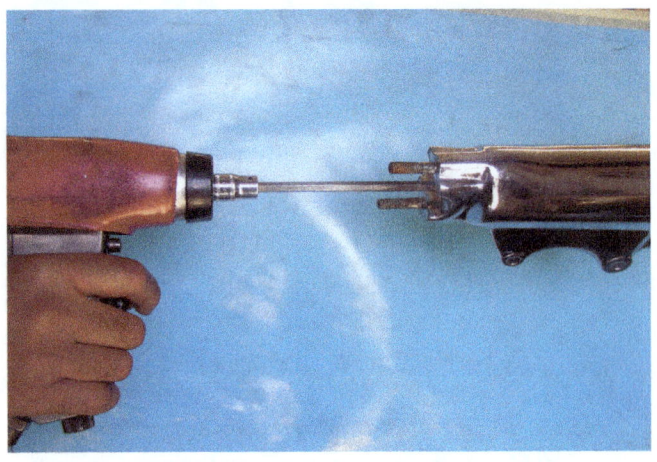

5. Tighten the retaining screw with a small air gun.

1. Here's the seal, and seal spacer, ready for installation with the help of the seal driver.

4. Use a measuring cup and a funnel to refill the slider assembly. Check with manufacturer for the proper amount of fluid.

2. The seal driver is used like a hammer to tap the seal into place.

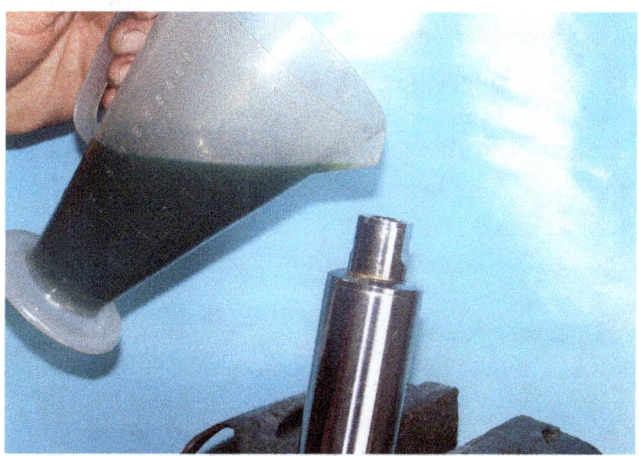

5. Pour the measured amount of oil into top of fork assembly. Some models must have the top screw removed.

3. Next, install the retaining ring which holds the seal and upper bushing in place.

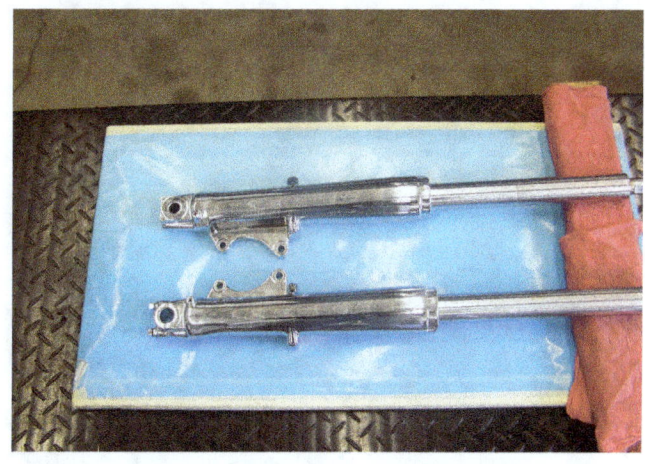

6. Here are the completed fork leg assemblies with chrome lower legs.

Neck Bearing Service

How it Works

The forks turn on a pair of tapered bearings, much like the wheel bearings used in many automobiles. Most late-model Harleys, and many aftermarket bikes, use the same bearing set.

Service

The neck bearings need periodic servicing. New style bearings have not changed in many years. When servicing the bearings use water proof grease. Bikes with springer-style front ends need to be serviced or changed more often than those with hydraulic fork assemblies. Check your manual for proper time and mileage service intervals. Also check for the pre-load specs and torque specs for your particular application.

When you disassemble the front end, be sure to inspect both the bearing rollers, and the bearing races. The bearing and bearing race should be replaced as a set.

Remove axle nut and lift front end just a small amount.

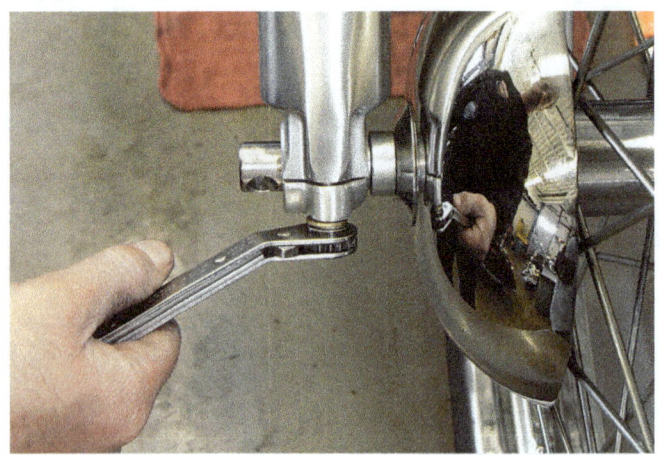

Remove the two 5/16 inch axle cap nuts from the right slider

Remove brake caliper and tie it off to the chassis with a wire tie.

Slide the axle out of the wheel. It should pull out easily. Some get corroded and need a little persuasion.

1. Wheel spacers sometimes come in different lengths. Pay attention to the original location.

4. Loosen the lower triple tree pinch bolts on both the right and left side.

2. Roll the wheel out from the front end.

5. Remove the top fork nut. The fork-tube assembly should now slide down and out.

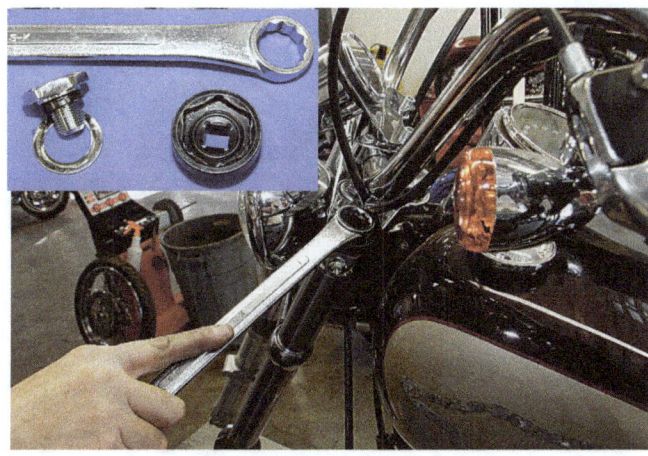

3. Loosen the top bolt from the fork slider. We use the special socket shown in the upper left.

6. The front brake hose is mounted to the triple tree. Remove the 2 hose mounts.

1. Remove the head lamp. Put it to the side, and cover with a towel.

2. The top nut cover is unscrewed from the top triple tree.

4. Once the top nut is off, cover the fuel tank and lift off the top triple tree. Slide it back and out of the way.

3. Tap down the lock tab and remove the top nut.

5. Remove the top pre-load nut and the top dust shield.

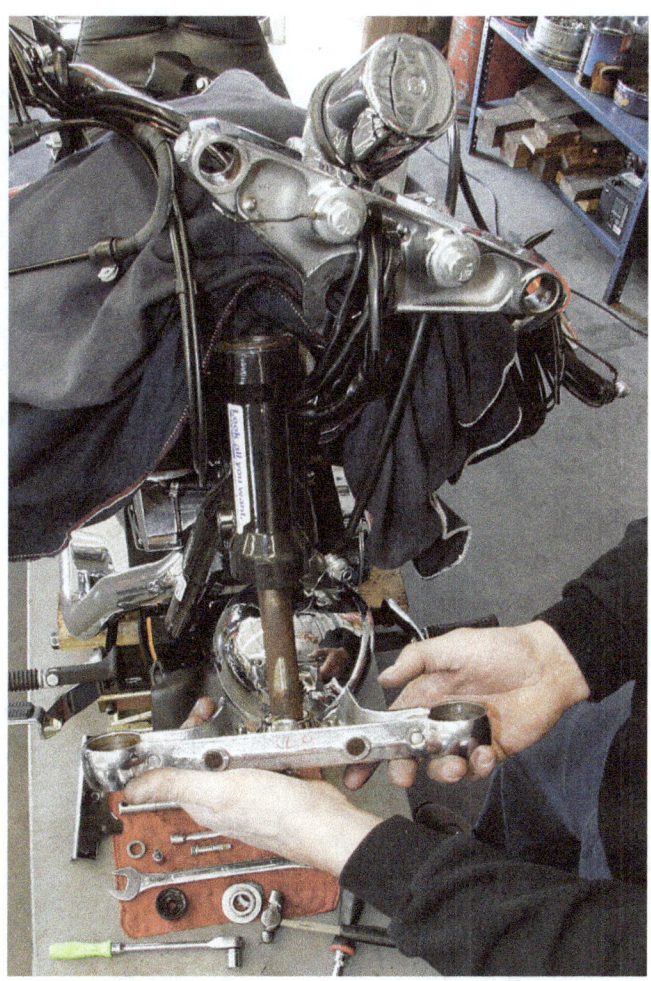

1. Slide out the lower triple tree.

3. Be sure the grease is pushed through the bearing. Continue packing until the grease is completely packed between all the rollers.

4. Put the repacked top bearing back in the neck.

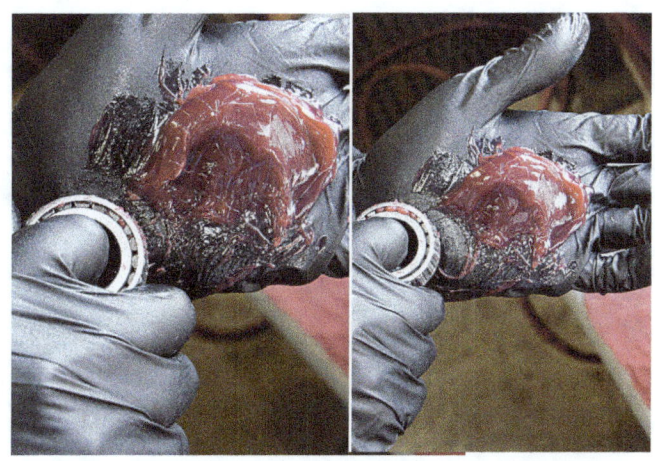

2. Hand packing: Place wheel bearing grease in your palm. Holding the bearing in your other hand force grease into the bearing until it is forced out of the top as shown.

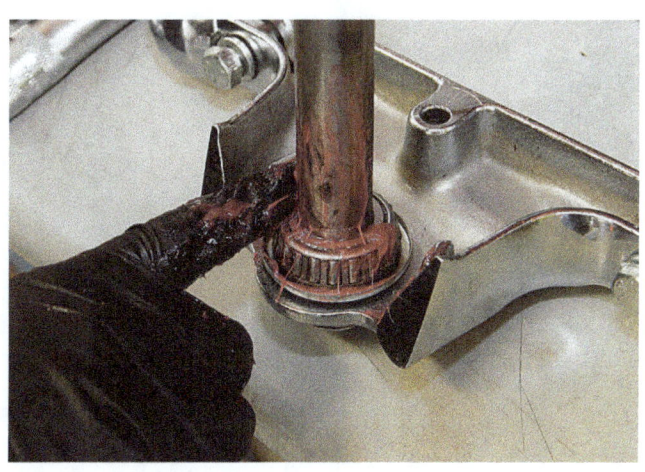

5. To pack the lower bearing you have to force grease in through the top of the bearing.

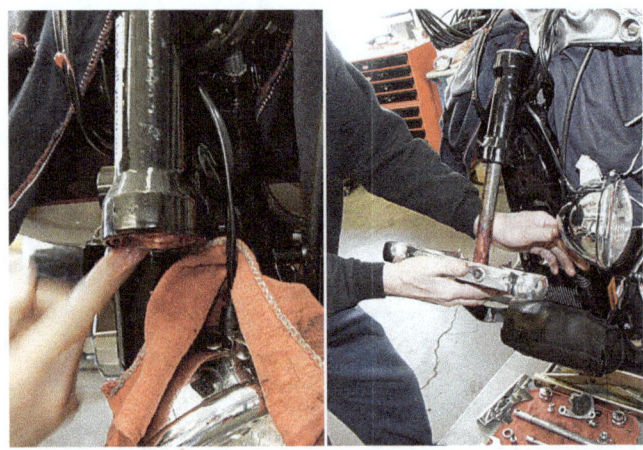

1. Apply liberal amount of grease to the bearing races before inserting the bearings. Slide the lower tree and stem into place.

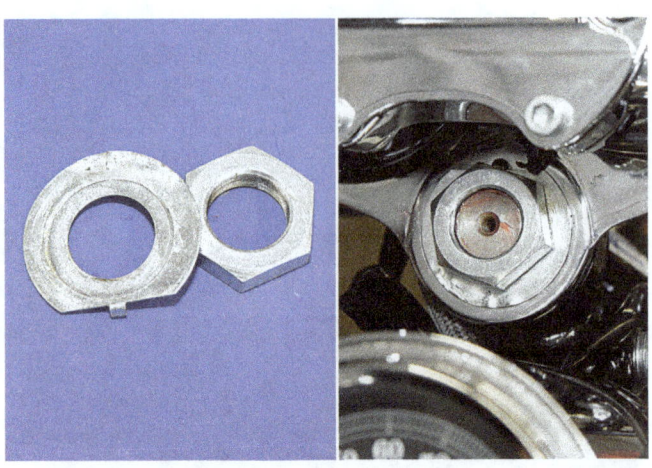

4. Install the lock tab and top nut. Do not torque down the nut yet.

2. Be sure the dust shield is in place. Install the pre-load nut and snug down to eliminate bearing play, but do not over-tighten.

5. Install the slider assemblies into trees and tighten top nut.

3. Place the top triple clamp back over the stem.

6. Assemble the wheel into sliders. Snug the axle nut onto the axle.

1. While holding the axle to prevent turning, torque the axle nut to 50 - 55 ft. lbs. Then torque the slider end cap nuts to 132 - 180 in. lbs.

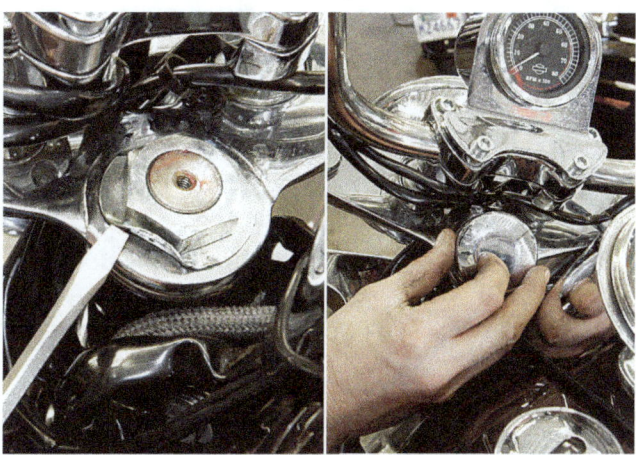

4. Bend over the lock tab on the top nut and re-install the top cover.

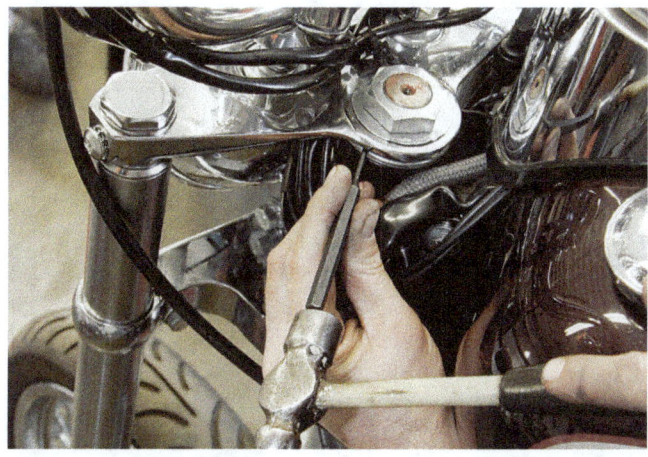

2. Do the final adjustment of the pre-load nut. You want a slight pre-load on the neck bearings but no binding. Check the service manual for specific recommendation.

5. Slide the caliper into place and install the bolts with blue Loctite on the threads.

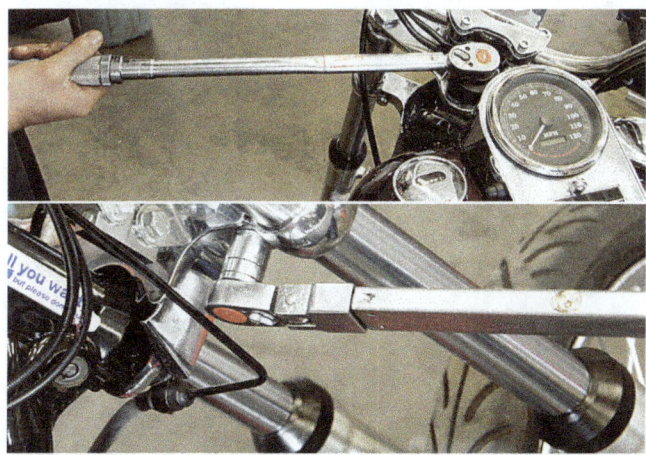

3. Torque the top tree nut to 50 - 65 ft. lbs. and torque the lower pinch bolts to 40 ft. lbs.

6. Torque the caliper mounting bolts to 25 - 30 ft. lbs. and mount the hardware. Be sure to pump up the brake lever before taking the bike off the hoist.

Chapter Eight

Shocks

Service and Replacement

Shock absorbers for motorcycles can be broken down according to the type of chassis they are designed to fit. Either they're meant for a Softail chassis, in which case they're hidden under the transmission, or else they're meant for the very traditional twin-shock suspension.

How They Work

Though the shock absorbers used on most motorcycles combine hydraulic damping and springs into one unit (this happens even with the front fork) it's easier to understand how each works by looking at the components separately.

A variety of shocks are available for both Softail and twin-shock frames. Before buying, decide what it is you want: Better handling, more adjustability or a lowered ride height.

Start with a spring that supports a weight. Compress the spring and let it go. It doesn't just bounce back to its original position, but rather goes well past that point and through a series of diminishing oscillations before coming back to the starting point. In order to dampen those oscillations a shock absorber (technically these are dampers not shocks) is used, often incorporated into the spring assembly. The first shock absorbers were just "friction" shocks rubbing a series of discs together to dampen the up and down movement of the springs. Hydraulic shocks are now standard equipment on all motorcycles. In place of friction between two discs, hydraulic dampers use the resistance of a non-compressible fluid to control the movement of the sprung portion of the shock absorber.

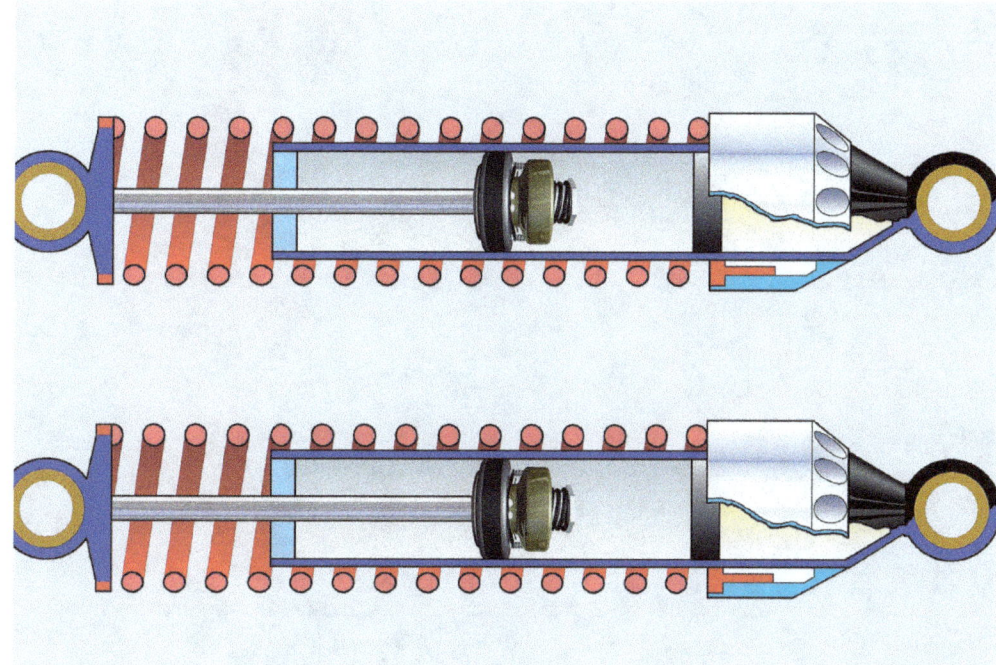

Cutaway illustration shows the damping plunger and the damping valves.

INSIDE THE SHOCK

Looking at a modern shock it's easy to imagine the piston attached to the pushrod, moving through a cylinder filled with oil. The viscosity of the oil, its quality and the size of the hole(s) that it passes through are the major factors affecting the stiffness of a particular shock absorber.

QUALITY ISSUES

As with every component on a modern bike, installing quality suspension components will ensure that the bike works as well as possible. Even shocks hidden from view

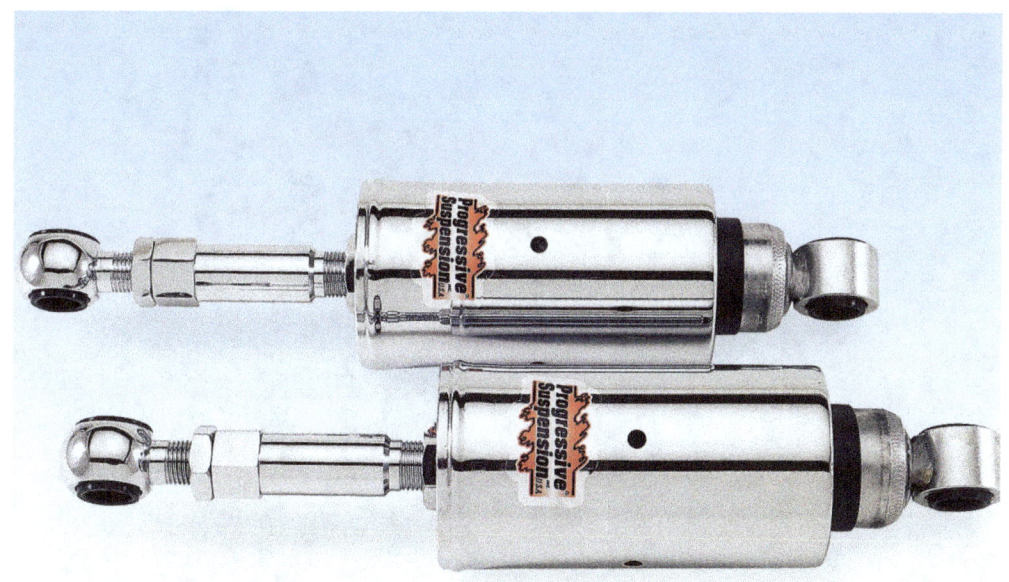

This early Softail shock set has a ride height adjustment at the shock end, and also a spring preload adjustment in the outside cover.

This demonstration frame shows how the shocks are mounted under the transmission in a Softail chassis.

should be the best quality you can afford.

As we said, fluid friction provides the damping in a modern shock absorber. A shock that works hard on a bumpy road will heat up as the result of that friction. Inexpensive shocks allow air to mix with the oil, and the oil itself, to change viscosity due to the heat. The net result is poor and inconsistent damping as the piston moves through an aerated froth of hot air and oil.

Inconsistent damping control and aerated oil are problems overcome by high quality shock absorbers. In a quality shock absorber all the components, from pistons to shafts, are larger and built to higher standards. The valves that control the damping are much more sophisticated to better handle a variety of road conditions and riding styles. To handle the heat, the amount of oil is increased. To diminish the heat the body of the shock is made of aluminum, which aids in the dispersion of heat. To prevent aeration of oil the shock is gas-charged, or filled with premium oil that won't change viscosity. The better shocks allow you to adjust the damping to compensate for your load or riding style.

Anatomy of a Spring

Coil springs are rated in weight/distance. For example, how many pounds of force does it

These Softail shocks have a bayonet type mount on one end as used on later model chassis. The wrench shown fits in the spring preload adjustment slots.

take to compress the spring one inch? You could take the coil springs for your shocks and test their ratings with a ruler and a scale.

The simplest springs are linear in their strength. That is, if 200 pounds will compress the spring one inch, then 400 pounds will compress the same spring two inches (up to a certain limit of course). Some springs are said to be "progressive" meaning the coils are wound tighter on one end than the other, which essentially creates a spring with a variable rate (this is typically in the twin-shock part of the market). On soft bumps you compress only the more tightly wound coils. On harsh bumps those coils "coil bind" quickly leaving you with a spring that is essentially much stiffer and better able to handle the larger bump. Nearly all shocks allow you to adjust the spring's preload to compensate for the rider's weight, or whether or not the bike is ridden two-up.

What to Buy
Shocks for Softails

The shock absorber layout on a soft-tail type bike is much different than on a twin-shock bike. When you ride over a bump the shocks of the soft-tail type suspension get longer, not shorter. For this reason the rear suspension needs an external "bump stop" instead of making the shocks do the job of limiting suspension travel on compression. Usually there are two rubber bumpers under the seat that provide a stop to the swingarm's travel.

Consider that Softails have less total travel than most twin-shock frames. As you reduce travel you make the shock's job, providing suspension control and a good ride, harder and harder.

Fitment

Softails from Milwaukee came with three slightly different rear suspensions. The first change came in 1989 and the next change came in 2000. When you buy shocks for your Softail, be sure you get the right ones.

Shocks for Twin-Shock Bikes

We've said it before, buy the best you can afford. When it comes to buying shocks for a twin-shock bike, there's more to the specifications than the length. In addition to the strength of the spring, the internal damping may be different between two shocks of equal length. So be sure to buy the shock meant for your make and model.

Spring preload can be adjusted on this shock by turning the detent ramp with the special wrench as shown.

Dyna Shock R&R

1. Taking the old shocks off this Dyna is easy. The lower fastener is a through bolt.

3. We are replacing the stock shocks with more sophisticated, fully adjustable shocks.

4. The new shocks come with inner bushings that must be used.

2. You need to have the bike supported as shown, now just pull the shocks off.

5. As always, torque the fasteners to the specs in your service manual.

Softail Shock R&R

1. Installing shocks in a Softail is more work than a twin-shock bike. We start at the back of the shock.

4. Put Loctite on the shoulder bolts.

2. On later model Softails, the front of the shock is a stud as shown. Note the way we support the bike.

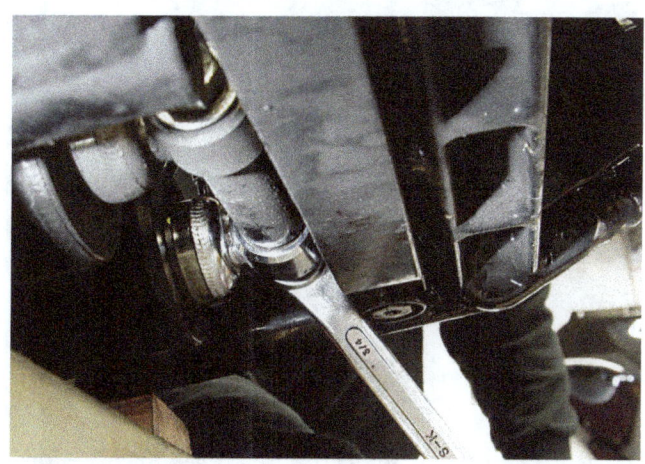

5. Access is poor, and getting the shoulder bolts tight requires patience.

3. With the rear shoulder bolt removed and the nut off at the front, the shock can be slipped out of the bike and the new one installed in its place.

6. Tightening up the nut on the front of the shock is last.

Softail Lowering Kit Install

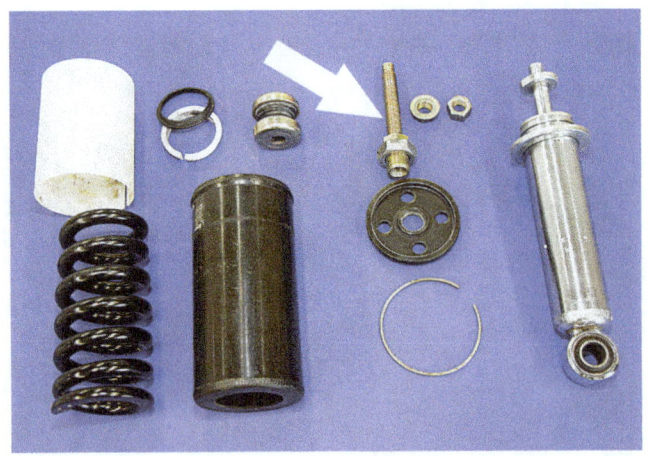

1. This is a typical Softail shock, disassembled, with the lowering kit.

4. Be sure the preload adjusting collar and the lowering kit are tight.

2. Red Loctite will make sure the shock doesn't come apart in service.

3. Installation of the lowering kit is next. By making the shock longer we lower the ride height.

5. With the lowering kit attached, we begin assembly of the shock.

1. This sequence shows various components and how they go together.

2. With the sleeve and collars in place, put the whole works inside the shock body.

3. You need a press to disassemble, and assemble the shock. This part is not for novice mechanics.

4. Compress the shock spring as shown...

5. ...until the preload collar is inside the body and you can fit the snap ring in place.

6. One stock shock and one "lowered" shock.

113

Chapter Nine

Tune-Up

Compression Test, Intake Gaskets & Cable Service

A tune up should be a whole lot more than just new plugs and an air filter. It is the time to go over the entire bike. In our opinion the following items should be part of every tune up on every bike:

1. Service the battery and cables.
2. Lube and adjust the throttle cables.
3. Clean the air box.
4. Service the air filter.
5. Check all motor-mount hardware and compo-

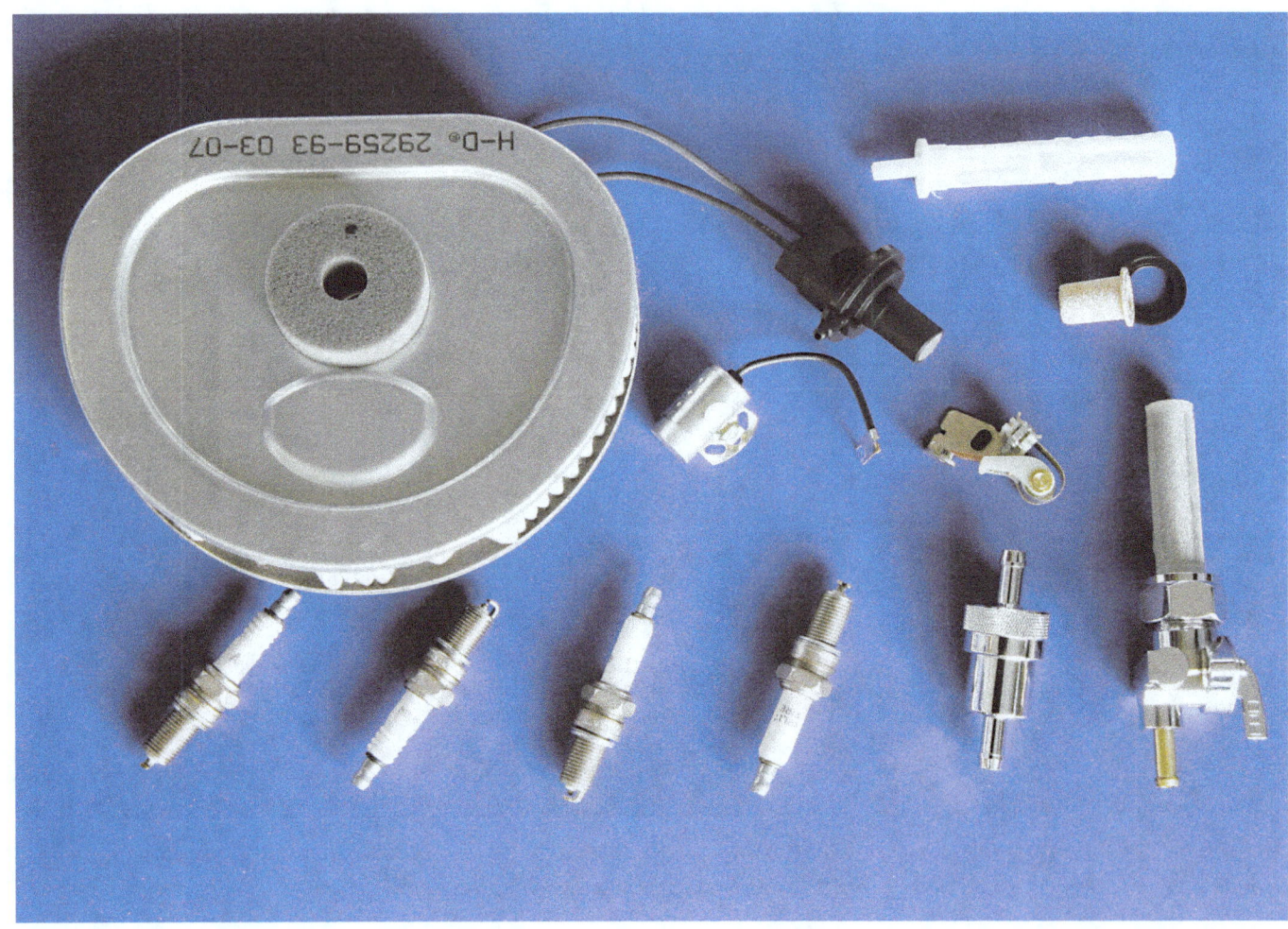

Shown are some of the parts commonly replaced during a tune up. The plugs and air filter are the most commonly replaced. Fuel filters and petcock screens should be cleaned on a regular basis. Only the older bikes use points.

nents, especially on rubber-mount bikes.
6. Check and clean the petcock screen on carbureted bikes.
7. Replace the points and condenser on older motorcycles.
8. Check the wiring and vacuum hose on the bikes equipped with a VOES switch.
9. The intake gaskets should be checked on bikes with runnability issues, or simply those with a number of miles on the odometer.
10. Take a look at all the fasteners, make sure none are loose.
11. Check the tension and condition of the final drive belt.
12. Adjust the primary chain.
13. Check the fluid reservoirs for the front and rear brakes, engine and transmission.
14. Check the condition of the brake pads.
15. Check the neck bearings by turning the bars slowly from side to side, there should be no roughness at any point.
16. Check the air pressure and condition of both tires.

When you're all done with the tune up and service, take the bike for a good road test to ensure every part of the machine works the way it should.

Remove plug with ratchet and socket.

Allow engine to cool off prior to removing spark plugs

Spark plugs come in different styles, sizes and heat ranges. Shown is a split fire (left) and conventional iridium.

115

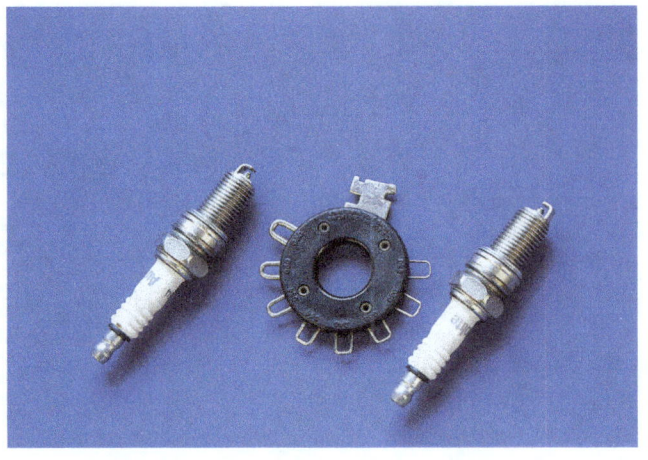

1. Spark plug with spark plug feeler gauge/adjuster

4. Use a small amount of lubricant on the threads prior to installing.

2. Most electronic ignition systems use a 042 gap. This must slide through the electrode and strap.

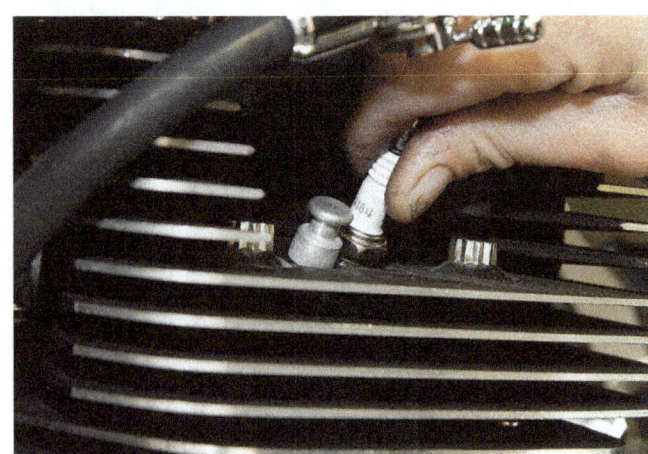

5. Screw in the plug by hand, then tighten until seated.

3. Use the tool to open the gap if needed. Lightly tap the strap down if gap is too wide.

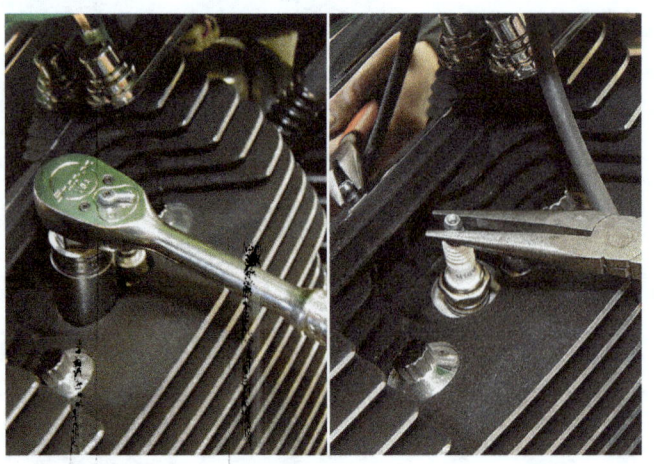

6, 7. Install the spark plug to the recommended torque. If the plug has a screw on cap, it's a good idea to be sure end-cap is tight on the plug.

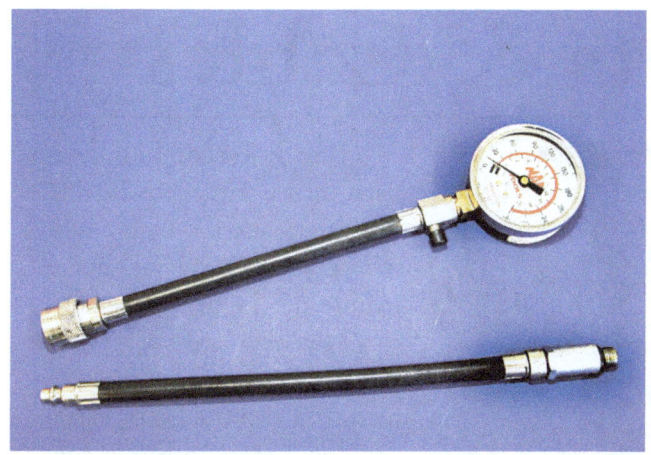

1. High quality compression testers come with a long hose to make installation easy on nearly any engine.

4. Hold throttle wide open when cranking the motor over. Turn the motor 5 to 7 compression strokes.

2. Screw spark plug adapter into plug thread until bottomed.

3. Good compression is a must for a properly tuned motor. It is always a good practice to test the compression when tuning the engine.

5. On a stock motor 90 psi is okay. 10% variance between cylinders is considered normal. Check for each motor's factory specification.

Intake Gaskets & Cables

The S&S teardrop air cleaner also acts as a carb support. This is a very common air cleaner, one of the standards of the industry.

With the filter and bracket assembly out of the way, the carb is easy to service or remove.

One of the common problems we see with both Harley and aftermarket V-twin engines is a vacuum leak at the intake manifold. The big rubber O-rings get hard and soon the perfect seal between the intake manifold and the heads is broken and a vacuum leak is the result.

To test for vacuum leaks at the intake manifold, start the motor and idle it at a low RPM. Spray WD-40 or CRC-56 on the intake manifold flanges (note the photos farther along in this chapter). If the idle smoothes out or the engine picks up speed, air is leaking past the seals and the intake manifold should be dismantled and serviced. Also check for a vacuum leak at the VOES switch and the hose on Evos, and the MAP sensor on Twin Cam equipped bikes.

When we disassembled the bike shown here, we decided to show more than just the replacement of the O-ring gaskets. We have taken time to identify each of the throttle cables, how they can be disconnected from the carburetor, and how they should be lubricated and adjusted.

If you service or replace either of the throttle cables, be sure that the routing is done in such a way that there are no kinks in the cable, and that you can turn the handle bars lock to lock without pinching the cable, or causing the engine to accelerate suddenly.

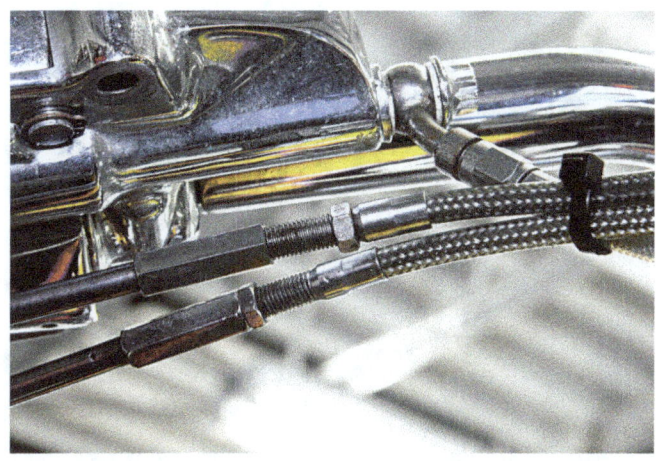

1. To remove the throttle cables from the carburetor you have to loosen the jam nut and back off the cable adjusters.

3. After removing the throttle cables from the throttle guides always check for frayed outer cables.

2. With the adjusters loose you can now remove the throttle cables from the throttle guide.

4. Make sure the fuel valve is shut off. Remove the fuel feed line to the carburetor.

5. On early models you will need to remove the ignition coil to gain access to the intake manifold mounting bolts.

1. Remove the two carburetor mounting bolts first. Make sure to hold on to the carburetor after the bolts are removed, the carburetor can fall off and be damaged easily.

2. After removing the ignition coil, you will have good access to the carburetor and the two back intake mounting bolts.

3. Remove the 4 intake manifold flange mounting bolts. Most factory bikes use Allen bolts.

4. With the bolts removed, slide the intake manifold forward and out.

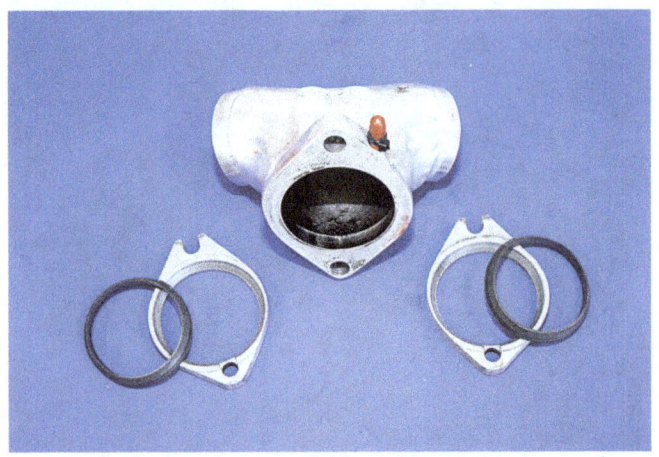

5. Here's the intake manifold with new O-ring seals. Make sure to check the mounting flanges - there is a front and rear marked with a F and R.

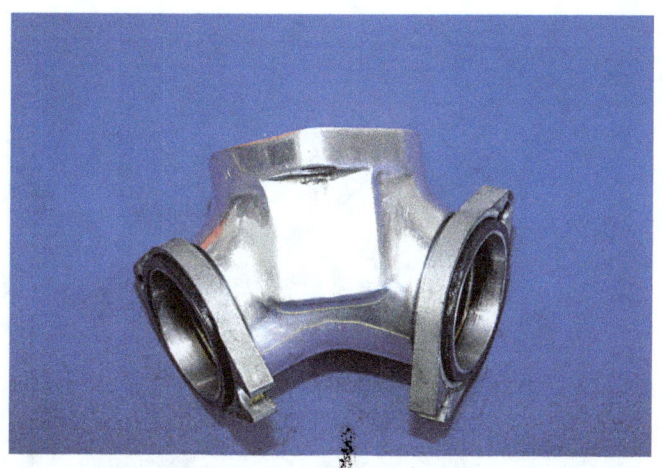

1. An intake manifold with the new O-rings ready to be installed.

2. Slide the intake manifold back into position. Make sure you start all four bolts first before tightening.

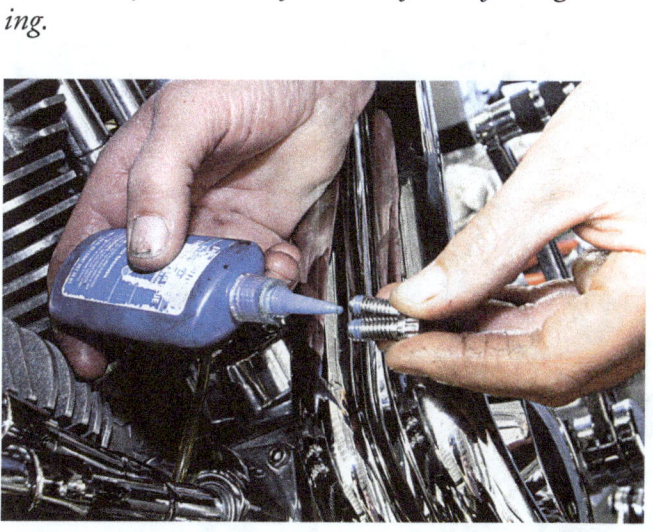

3. Clean the bolts and apply blue Loctite and tighten the four bolts evenly.

4. Now hold the carburetor in place and start both carburetor mounting bolts first before tightening. Be sure to tighten both bolts evenly.

5. Reinstall the two throttle cables into the throttle guide.

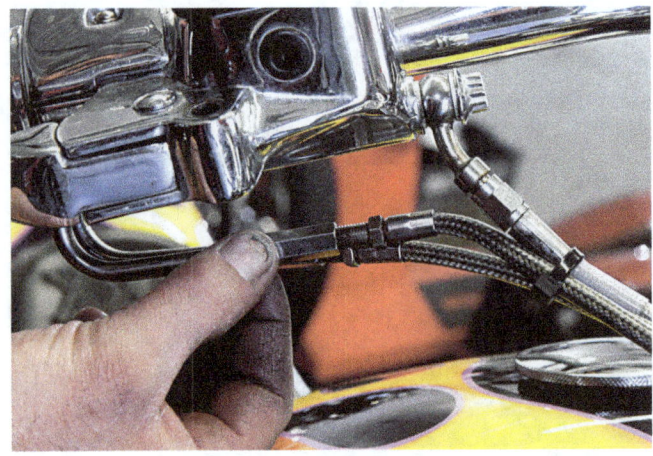

1. When adjusting the throttle cables, be sure the carburetor has full throttle, and goes to idle without any binding.

2. To lubricate the cables, start by removing the top of the throttle housing.

4. Here we are lubricating the idle cable.

5. And here we're applying the lube to the throttle cable. In this case we are using WD-40 as the lubricant.

Reinstall the air filter inner mounting plate. On S&S models be sure to line up the choke. Always Loctite the inner-plate mounting bolts. If they come loose they can fall into the motor while it is running!!!!

Always replace or clean the air filter element before reinstalling.

Tighten the outer mounting bolts evenly after coating them with a little Loctite blue.

Carburetors

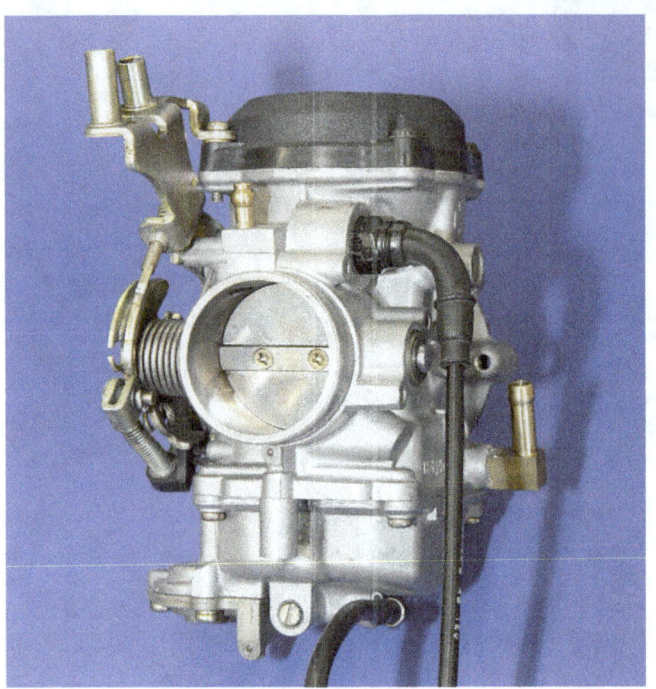

Used on hundreds of thousands of Harleys, the Keihin carburetor is both very durable and easily serviceable.

How it Works

There will always be carburetors. Older bikes, customs and high performance bikes will all continue to use carburetors, and for anyone who rides one of these motorcycles, a little carburetor knowledge is a necessity.

Carburetors need service and periodic adjustment. They collect sediment in the fuel bowl, and evaporating fuel often leaves behind a varnish-like residue that hangs up moving parts such as floats, the needle and seat, accelerator pump, and check balls. Which is why the carb may need to be cleaned later if a bike was stored without having the fuel drained properly first (see Storage chapter).

Most carbs have four circuits: idle, slow, main and enrichment. Any of these circuits can be modified or tuned. With the Keihin carbs, be sure the slide diaphragm rubber is in good condition, it can often be burned by back-firing into the carb, caused by a lean mixture or vacuum leak where the intake manifold meets the cylinder heads.

Once you are familiar with the components, servicing a carburetor is a very straight forward procedure. Dynojet and others have available recalibration kits designed to improve performance. These hop-up kits are available for all the popular carbs. Kits for the Keihin carb come with an emulsion tube, a lighter slide spring, needles, jets, necessary drills, and a good instruction sheet. We have used these kits with great success.

Carbs can be tuned to work extremely well, but in our opinion fuel injection can be mapped to run at all RPMs, load conditions and temperatures. It's simply hard to match the precision and flexibility of a good fuel injection system with a carburetor.

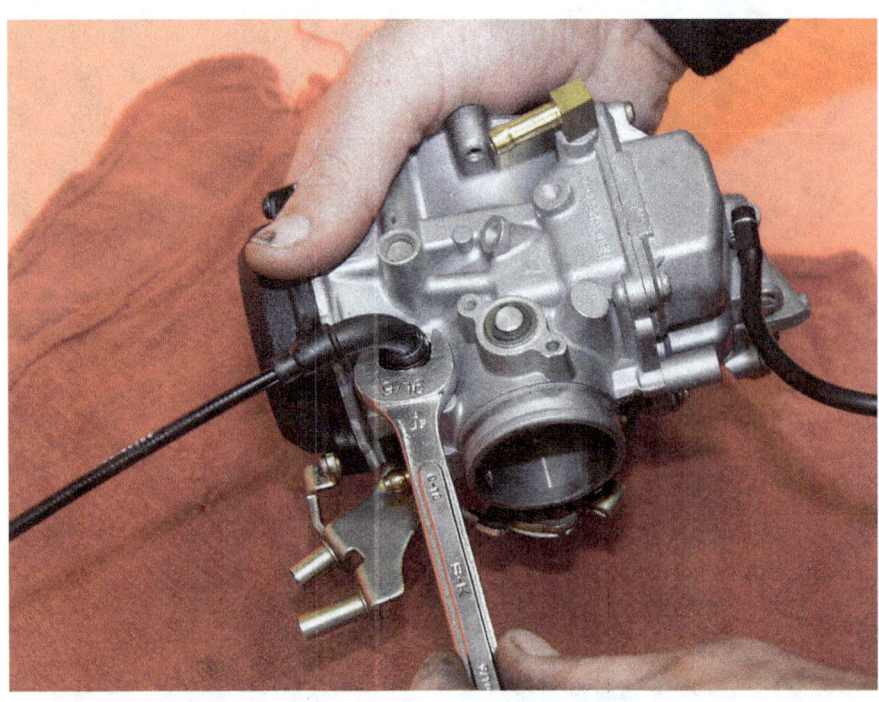

To start, unscrew the fuel enrichment cable. Be sure to drain the fuel from the carburetor before starting service or repairs.

Keihin Carburetor Service

1. Remove the top cover. Start with the throttle linkage bracket.

2. Sometimes the side bracket screws are difficult to remove, if so use a small vice grip to break them free.

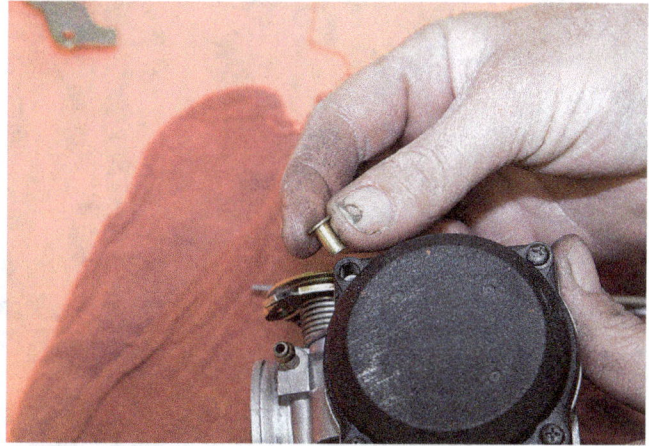

3. The top right corner uses a brass sleeve under the screw so as not to crack the plastic cover when tightening.

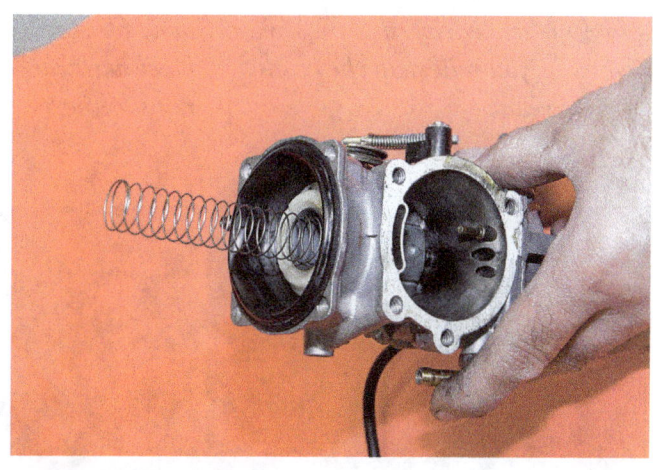

4. With the cover off, the spring and diaphragm are exposed. Now slide out the spring and slider assembly.

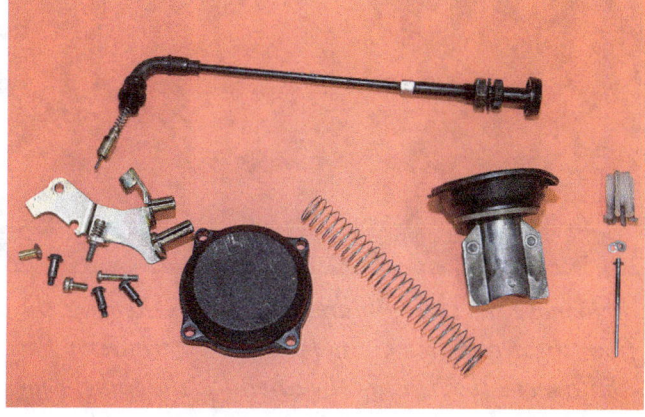

5. Parts from the top half of carburetor are spread on the bench. Be sure the diaphragm is not ripped or torn.

125

1. Remove the four Phillips screws from the carburetor bowl. Make sure your screwdriver fits the screws tightly or you will strip the heads of the screws.

2. Remove the carburetor float bowl. Make sure to look inside the bowl for dirt and debris. Clean the bowl with carburetor cleaner before reinstalling.

3. The accelerator dump rod is now loose, remove it from the hole in the lever at the side of carburetor body.

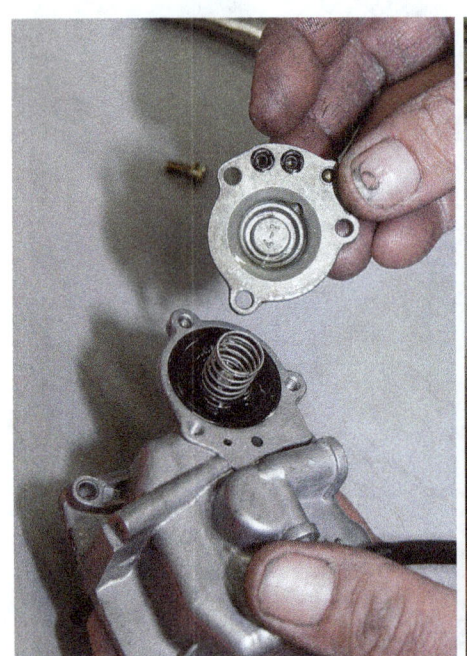 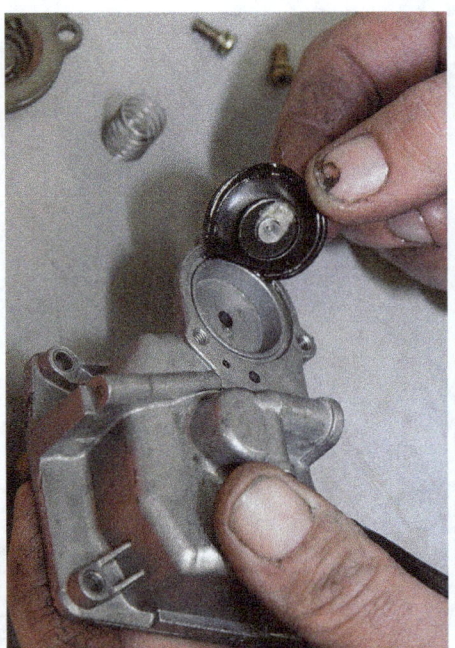 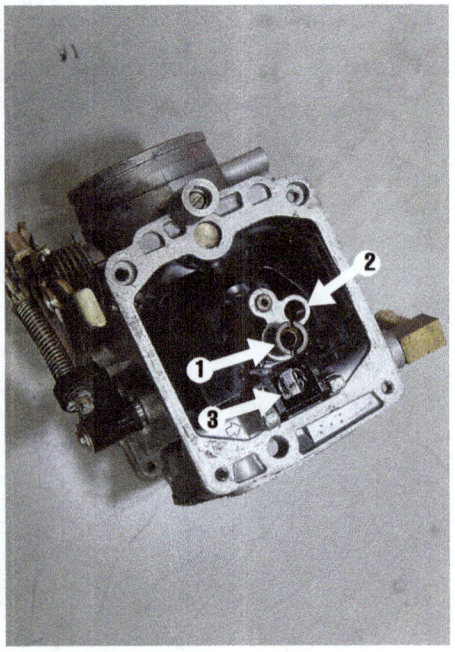

4. Remove the three Phillips screws from the accelerator pump housing and remove the housing. Be careful not to lose the spring and O-rings.

5. Remove the diaphragm from the carburetor bowl. Check the diaphragm for cracks or splits in the rubber.

6. Here are the:
#1. Needle jet holder
#2. Slow jet hole
#3. Float needle and seat

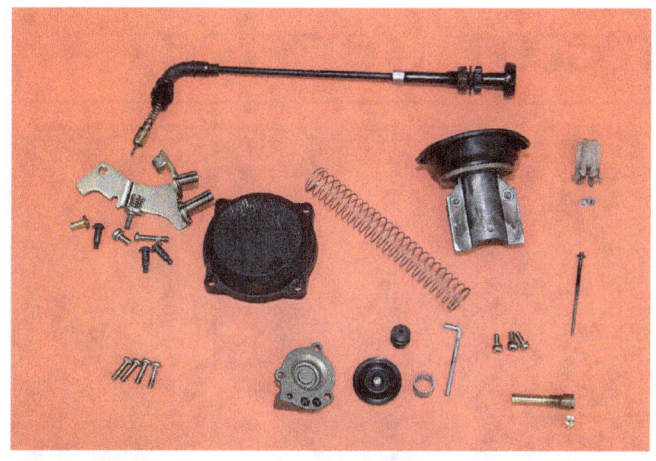

1. Here's a blow up of the carburetor disassembly so far.

4. Removing the float pin, make sure the punch is not larger than the float pin. Hit punch lightly with hammer to remove the pin.

2. With the needle jet holder removed, be careful not to lose the tube, pointed out above.

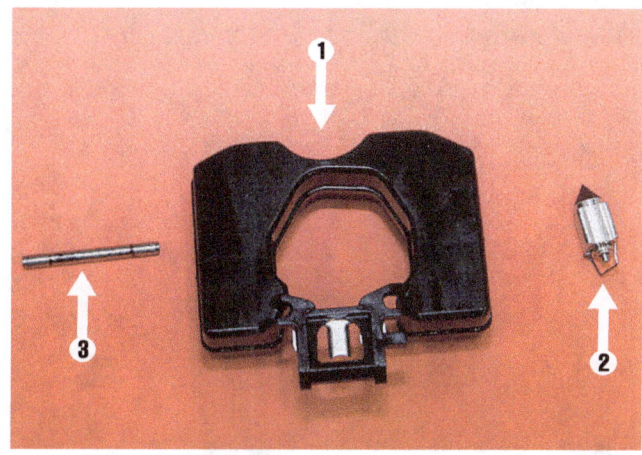

5. Here are the:
#1. Float
#2. Fuel valve (needle) and clip. #3. Float pin

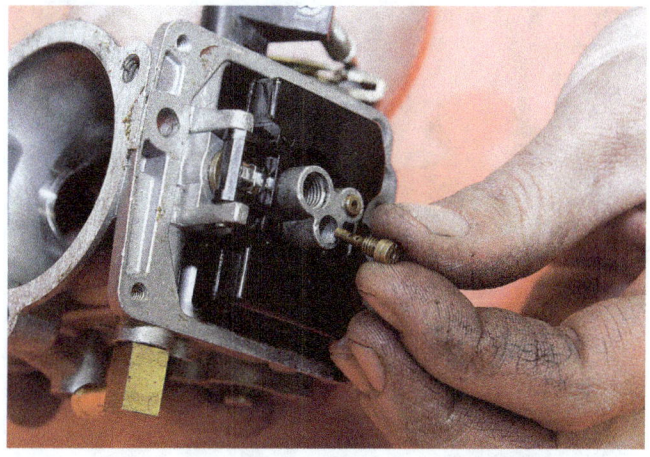

3. Here's the slow jet removed from the carburetor body. The main jet and jet holder were already removed from the carburetor.

6. This is the fuel drain. Remove the drain screw, clean out with carburetor cleaner and blow out with air.

Mikuni Carburetor Service

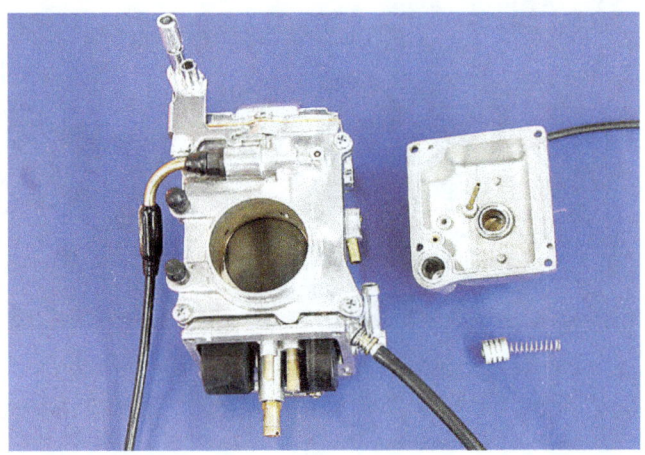

2. Mikuni carburetor with the float bowl removed. Note the accelerator plunger and spring

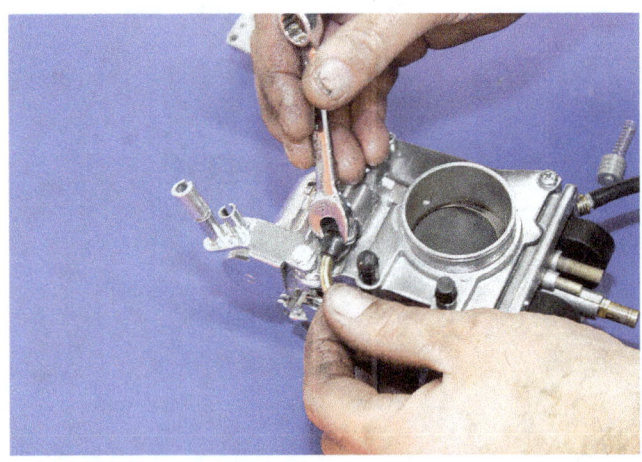

3. Remove the choke cable from the body of the carburetor.

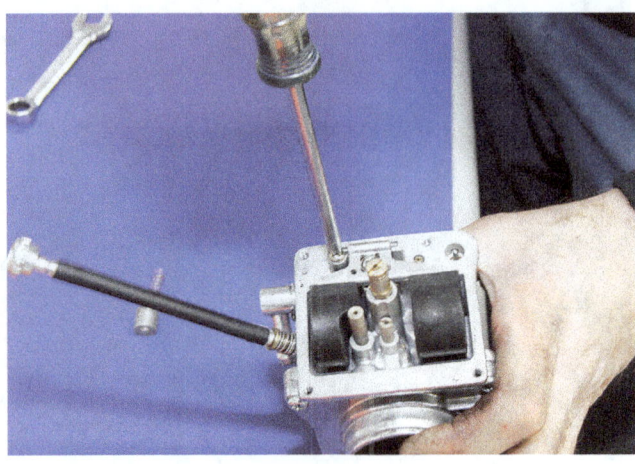

4. Next, remove the float pin lock screw, slide out float pin, and remove float and needle valve.

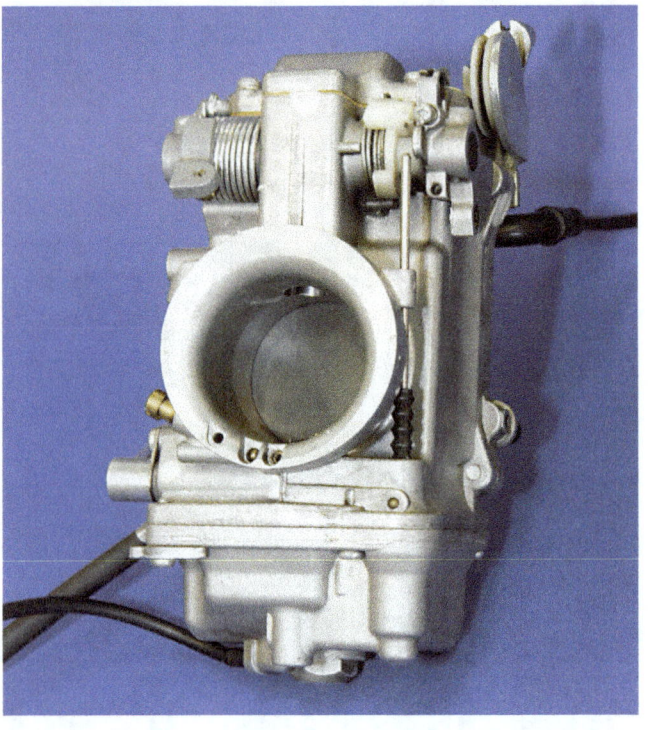

1. Unlike the Keihin, the Mikuni has no vacuum diaphragm or vacuum controlled needle.

5. Carburetor with the float removed. Remove main jet and clean with carb. cleaner or compressed air.

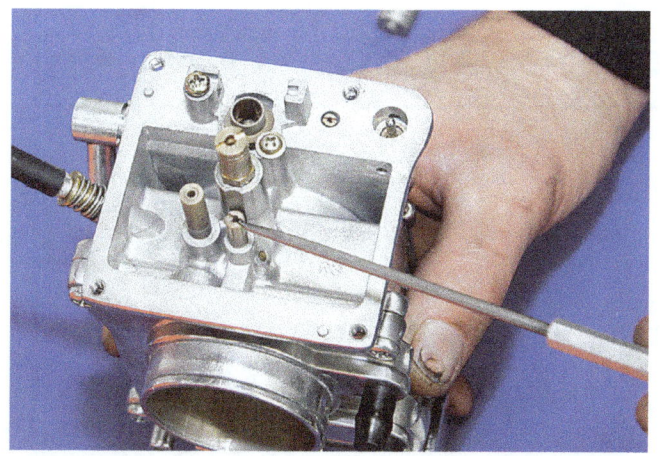

1. Also remove the pilot jet. Clean with choke spray or compressed air.

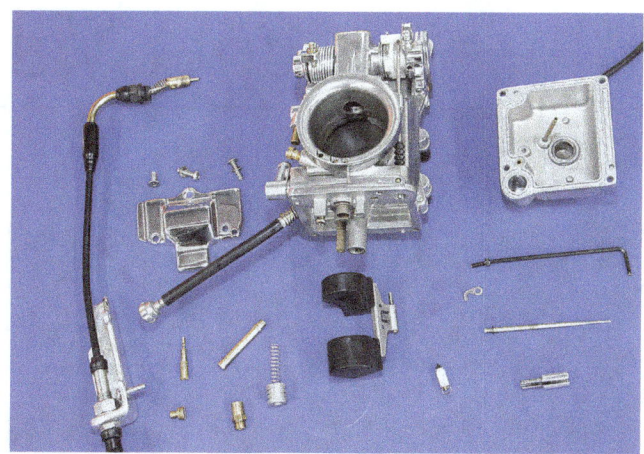

4. This is the disassembled carburetor.

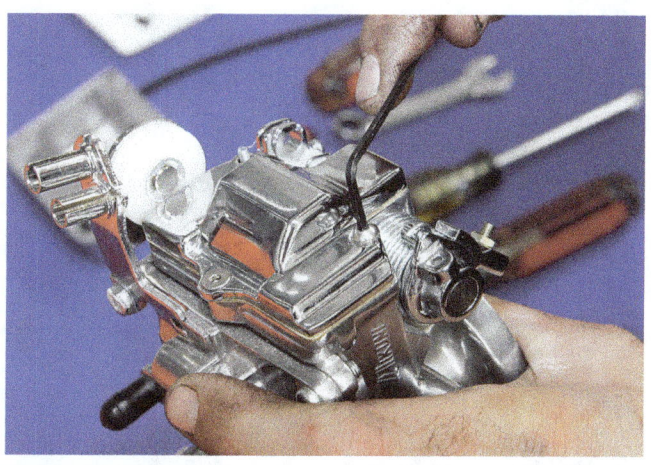

2. Remove the top cover to gain access to the needle jet and slide assembly.

5. Reassembly means reinstalling the needle jet, the lock clip, then the screw that holds the clip in place.

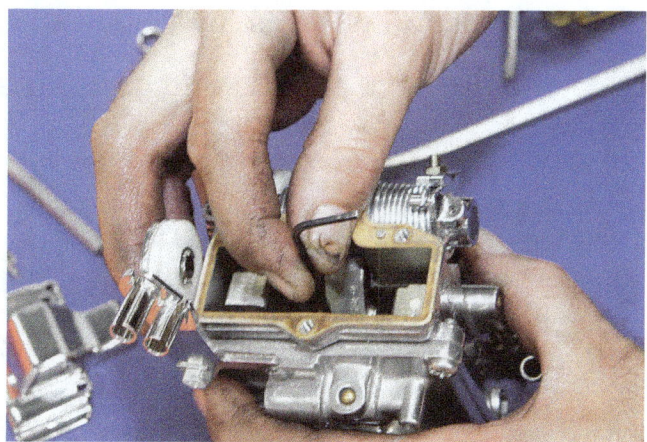

3. Use a 2.5 mm Allen wrench to loosen the needle jet lock clip. Swing clip to the side and remove the needle jet. Be careful not to lose the needle jet washer or lock clip.

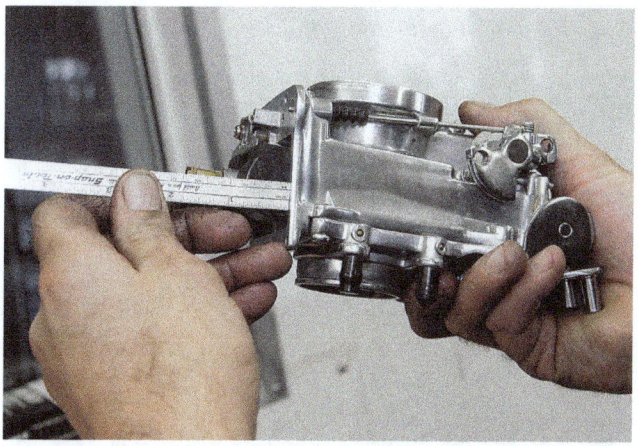

6. To set float level, hold the carburetor horizontal until the float touches the needle valve. Measure the float height from base of carb. to top of float. Should be 18mm + or - 2mm. Bend the float tab to change.

Fuel Valve Service

1. To start, drain the fuel from the bike completely, into an approved container.

2. To remove the fuel valve use a one-inch wrench. The center nut is a right-handed thread on top and a left-handed on the bottom.

3. Use a shop rag when removing the valve. Some fuel will leak out. Be careful with the leaking fuel, a spark can cause a fire.

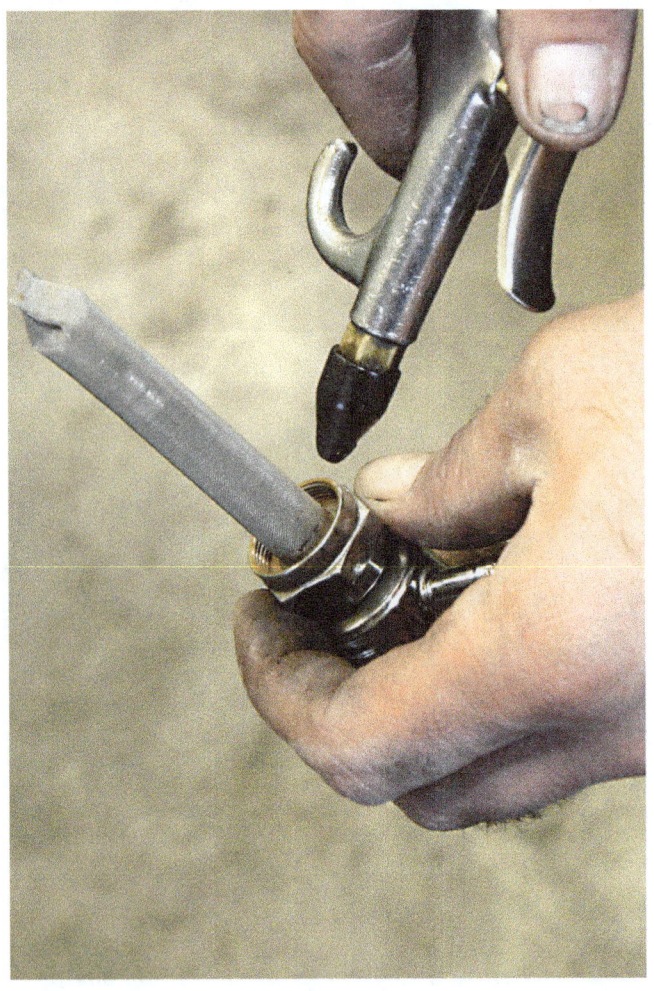

4. Rust and dirt build up on the screen and can block fuel flow to the carburetor. Blow off the fuel screen and clean with choke cleaner and compressed air.

5. With the petcock reinstalled, we attach the fuel line, clamp it in place, fill the tank with gas and check for leaks.

VOES - Vacuum Operated Electric Switch

How it Works

The VOES switch advances or retards the engine timing depending on the load, as indicated by the amount of vacuum in the intake manifold. At low vacuum readings, like full throttle acceleration, the switch is open and the timing is retarded. Once you're up to speed and cruising under light load, the vacuum is much higher, which closes the VOES switch and sends a signal to the ignition module that the engine can take advantage of more timing advance - which will enhance mileage and response to part-throttle acceleration. Checking the operation of a VOES switch is pretty simple, as shown below. Always be sure the vacuum line is in good condition, and not cracked or broken.

The VOES switch is mounted under the motor mount and senses vacuum through a hose that runs to the intake manifold. Check for a broken or cracked vacuum hose.

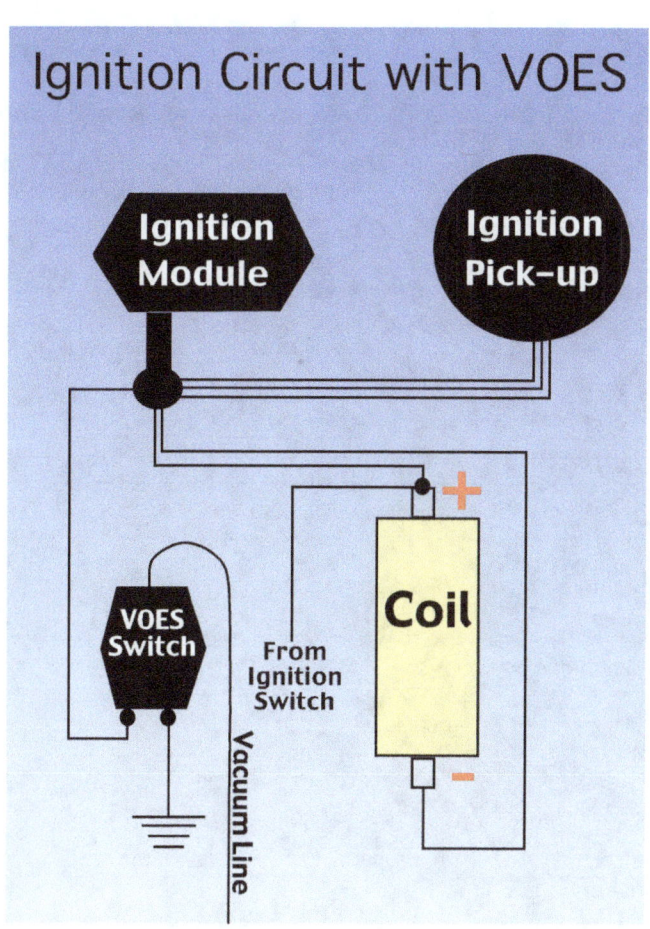

The basic VOES circuit.

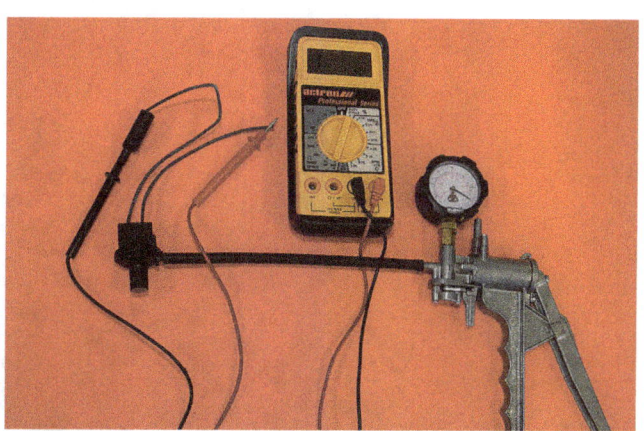

You can check the operation with a vacuum pump and ohmmeter. Low vacuum opens the switch and retards engine timing to prevent detonation.

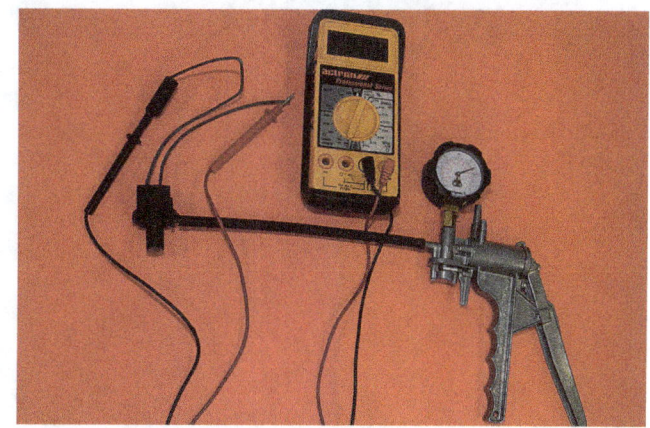

High vacuum closes the switch which grounds the wire from the ignition module, which in turn advances the timing to help fuel mileage and throttle response.

Chapter Ten

Storage

Put Your Baby Away for the Season

Stable temperature and low humidity are a must if you want to keep your cycle from corroding or rusting while it sits in storage. Preparation for storage is important, partly because modern fuels can go bad or "bounce" during storage and plug up the fuel system later. A small amount of time spent before you put the bike away will prevent problems months later when you try to start the bike up again.

At our shop we like to drain all the fuel from

You don't want to just stick the bike in the corner of the garage for the winter. Take time to make sure that no damage occurs during that long winter sleep, and find a winter home with low humidity and a constant temperature.

the tank, and the carb or fuel injection system. We use the fuel we've taken out in another vehicle and then start the bike up with fresh gas in the spring.

Draining the fuel from the tank is a little more work than is was a few years ago. Most of the bikes now have vacuum-operated petcocks, which means in order to drain all the fuel on a carbureted bike you need a vacuum pump (shown nearby) to activate and open the fuel valve.

Even though our storage areas is heated and dry, we like to pull the plugs, squirt a little oil in the cylinder and then turn over the engine so we know the rings and cylinders are coated with engine oil.

Motorcycle batteries don't always last very long, and part of the reason for that is the fact that riders don't keep them charged during the winter months. You can't just put a trickle charger on a battery and leave it there, eventually it will overcharge the battery. We like to hook our storage bikes up to a Battery-Tender type charger.

If you hook up the leads that come with the charger to the battery, then it's just a matter or plugging the unit into the bike and then into a wall socket.

You don't want your bike to deteriorate during the winter. And you do want them to fire right up in the spring. The way to guarantee both outcomes is to take the time to store the bike correctly.

To start, you want to drain the fuel tank. Cut the fuel line clamp and remove the hose.

Locate the vacuum diaphragm on the fuel valve and remove the vacuum hose.

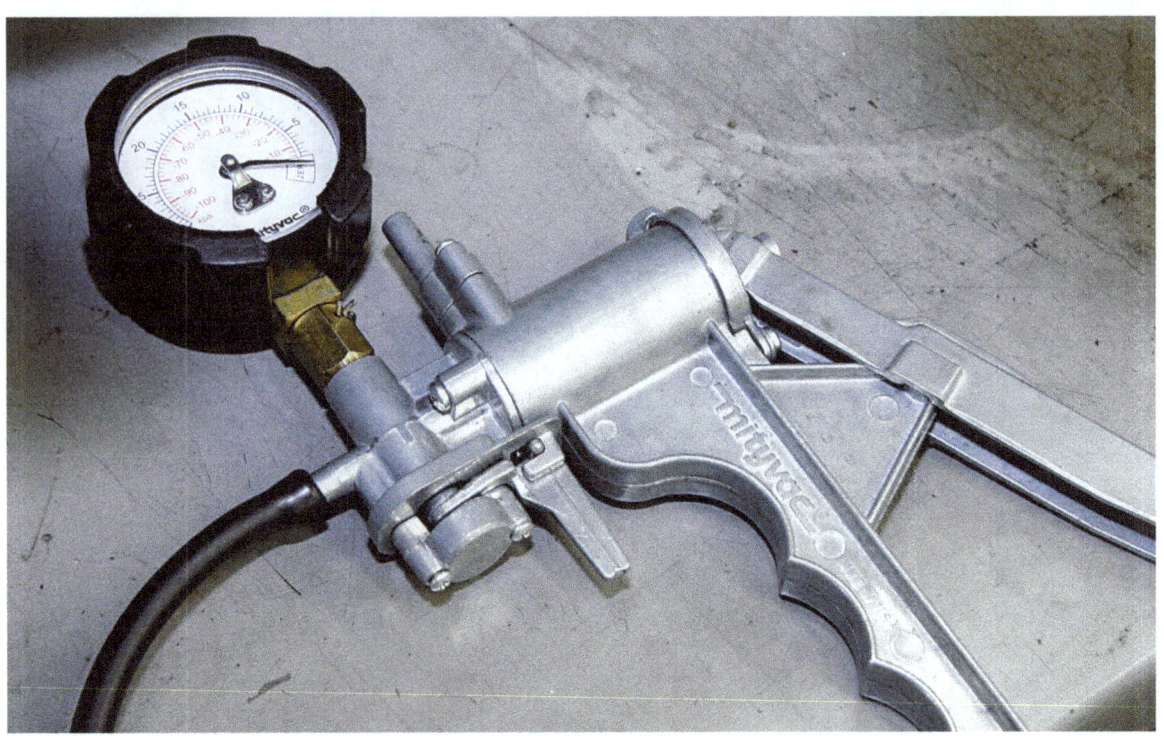

A handheld vacuum pump is needed to open the fuel diaphragm valve on later model bikes with vacuum controlled fuel valves.

Connect the vacuum pump to the fuel valve and connect a gas line that can be used to drain the gas tank.

1. Use a vacuum pump to open the fuel valve. Set the valve on reserve and drain fuel into approved container.

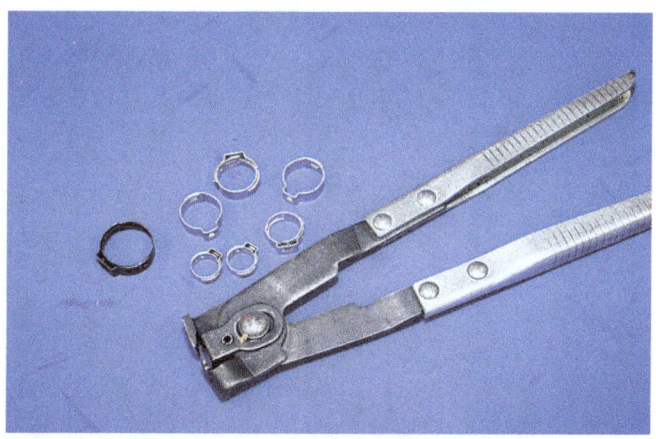

2. Use the correct clamp and pliers to reinstall the fuel line. Clamps come in various sizes, be sure to use the correct size.

3. Once all the gas is drained, reinstall and clamp the gas line.

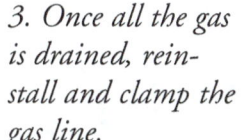

4. Some carburetors have a drain screw that can be opened to drain all the fuel from the float bowl. (See the Tune Up chapter.)

135

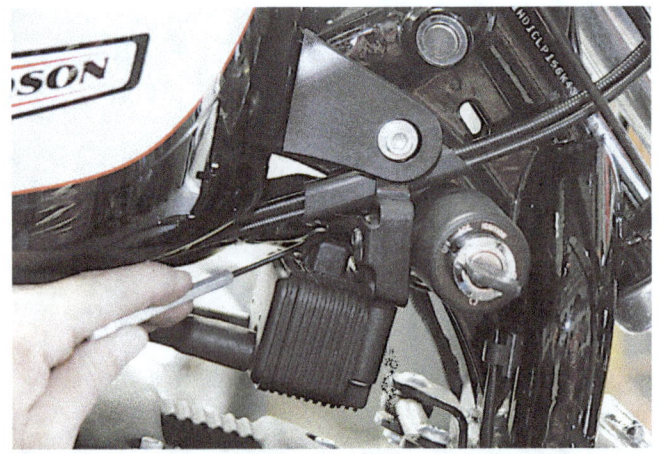

1. Locate the power source to the ignition coil.

3. Remove the spark plugs.

2. Disconnect the power source to the ignition coil to avoid any sparks when the engine is cranked over.

4. Use 20/50 motor oil, pump 4 or 5 squirts into each cylinder, crank the engine over to lube and protect the cylinder and piston rings during storage.

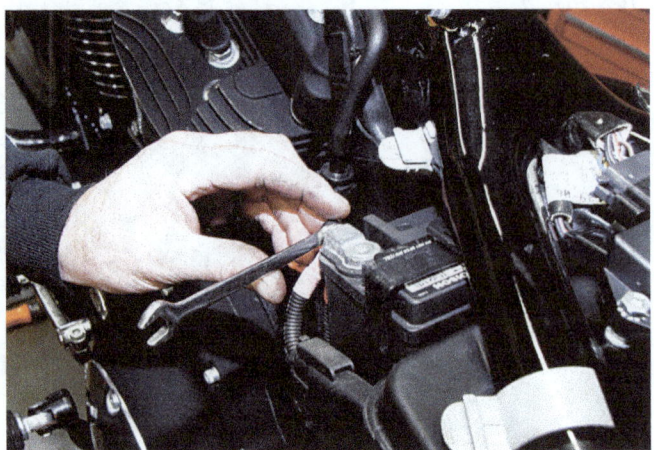

5. Disconnect the battery prior to storage, (be careful not to short the positive terminal to ground,) or attach a battery tender, (see next page).

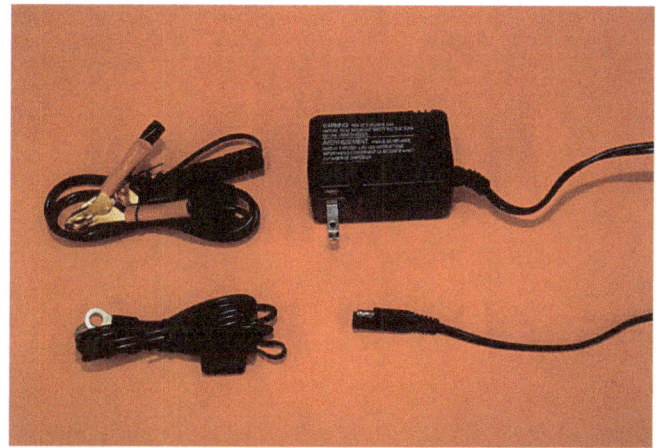

1. Battery tenders are easy to install and will keep the battery charged when the bike is not in use.

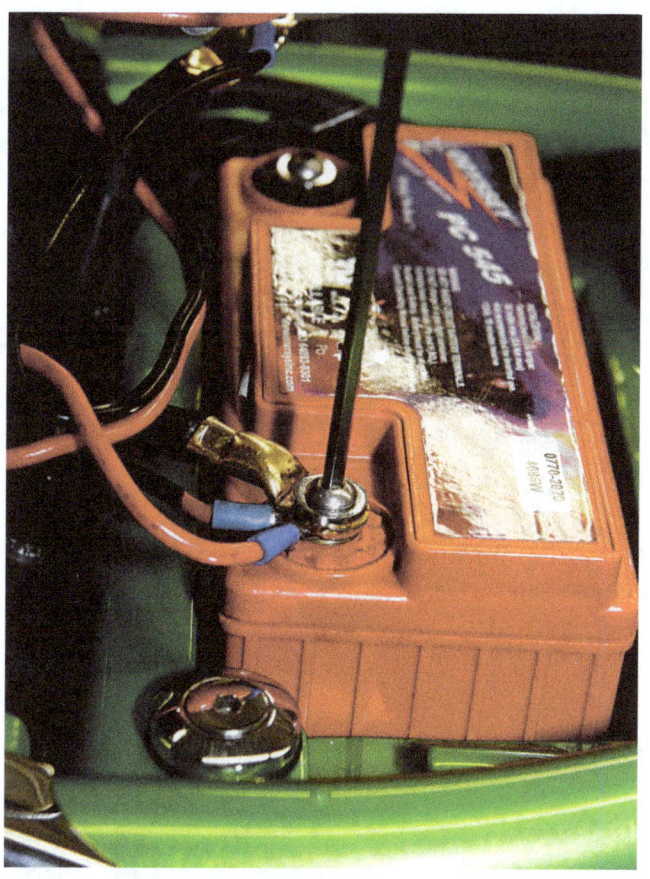

2. Attach the battery tender wires to the battery, red is positive, black is negative.

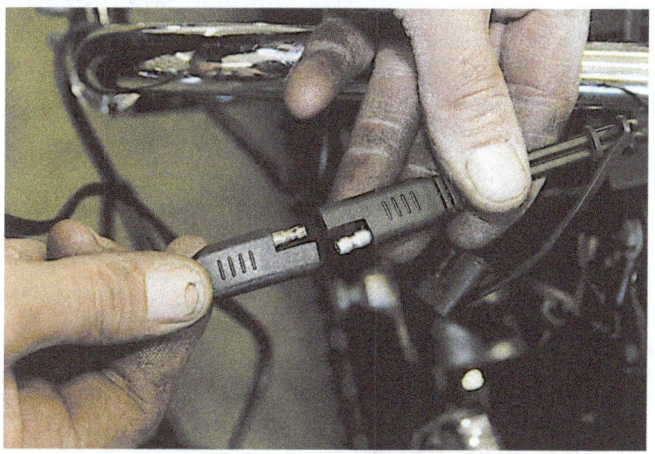

3. Install the plug connector in an easily accessible spot.

4. Battery tenders can be connected to the battery all winter long. These are better than the old trickle chargers because they will not overcharge the battery.

Chapter Eleven

Dyno

What you should get from your Dyno Test

WHAT IT IS

Technically, a dynamometer is used to measure torque. From torque and rotational speed, horsepower can be calculated. The dyno's "brake" or load unit, is used to create a certain engine load condition. Modern units such as the Dynojet model 250I are equipped with an air-fuel meter, which is used to measure the ratio of oxygen to fuel. High-flow fans, used to keep the engine cool during testing, are part of any good chassis dyno.

On all the bikes we run on the dyno, the air-fuel ratio is the most common adjustment needed.

So many people have their bikes dyno tested these days that we decided to try and take the mystery out of the dyno, and explain what you should get out of a standard dyno test.

On a carbureted bike the ratio is changed by changing jets, needles, needle height and accelerator pump adjustments. With fuel injection, we are able to change part of the map that controls how much fuel the engine receives under a certain set of speed and load conditions. Generally, we make only one adjustment and then we retest the bike to make sure there is an improvement in the areas where we are concentrating.

The ignition timing can also be checked and set during a dyno run. We will often note the power output, then advance or retard the timing, and retest the bike to check the power output after the timing change.

The probe for the air-fuel meter must be slipped far enough up into the muffler that the exhausts sample is not contaminated with fresh air.

MANY USES FOR A DYNO

The dyno is a great tool for checking a new or rebuilt motor. You can run the engine on the dyno under a light load, then check for oil leaks, oil pressure, engine temperature, detonation and overall running condition. We feel any new motor should not have full-power pulls until the motor is broken in. The dyno is a great way to do the initial break in. Your owner's manual or engine builder will have more information on what constitutes full break in.

Other things can be checked on the dyno as well. Like the clutch, is it slipping under full power? And the speedometer, is it calibrated correctly?

When we assemble a bike it is very helpful to run the bike before it goes out on

The dyno operator has a number of "screens" available, including the typical horsepower/torque graph with air-fuel line at the bottom, or a tachometer and speedometer.

The screen on the right shows the torque and horsepower curves, with the fuel mixture readings on the lower graph. On the left is the fuel table, by changing the numbers in the table you change the fuel mixture.

At this point we are preparing to make another run. It's important to warm the bike up first and make sure the gauges are working. Note the speedo and tachometer on the right hand screen and the air-fuel graph on the far right.

the road to check the general operation and to seat in all the components in a controlled environment.

TYPICAL DYNO TEST

We start the test by entering the person's name, the make and model of their bike, and any modifications or problems the customer is having with the bike. This is the beginning of the file. The motorcycle is put on the dyno and strapped down, the exhaust probe is inserted in to the muffler, and the computer is attached to the bike's data port. Before starting the bike, the dyno operator takes an overview of the bike. We note things like tire condition, any oil or fuel leaks, and the brake and clutch operation. If everything checks out OK, the bike is started and several warm up cycles are run to bring the motor and transmission up to operating temperature.

Once it's warm, three wide-open pulls are done. Then we analyze the air fuel ratio to make sure the motor isn't to too lean or too rich. Next we do several quarter throttle and half throttle pulls, and the fuel mixture is looked at again. Now we make any necessary changes to air-fuel ratio or timing, and retest.

When the dyno test is complete and all adjustments are made, the customer should get a horsepower and torque graph that shows the before and after torque and horsepower curves. The same paperwork should include a before and after fuel curve.

REAL WORLD TESTS

Both of the bikes noted below (the dyno graphs can be seen on the right) came to us with the engine work already done and the aftermarket parts installed. In both cases the shop that did the work installed generic maps (aka downloads) that were supposed to provide correct fuel and ignition maps for that particular combination of parts. The gains we achieved were accomplished with careful tuning. Basically we built a new map for each bike.

Test&Tune #1

Ron Benard's bike is an 88 inch Twin Cam with aftermarket exhaust and air filter, and a Power Commander.

The original fuel and ignition map is a generic down load that produced readings of 59.65 horsepower and 70.02 ft. lbs. of torque. You will note that the fuel line indicates a rich condition. After re-mapping the bike and doing a series of pulls, the fuel line is good and the horsepower is up to 69.82 and torque is up to 77.77 ft. lbs. That's a gain of 10.17 hp and 7.75 ft. lbs. of torque plus an increase in fuel mileage and throttle response.

Test&Tune #2

James Shapiro's bike is a 95 cubic inch Twin Cam with flat top pistons, minor cylinder head porting, slip in camps, aftermartket exhaust, air filter and a power commander.

If you look at the original map, you see the bike is extremely rich up to 2800 RPM, and then it goes lean. The initial horsepower is 69.65 and the torque is 88.9 ft. lbs. After re-mapping the fuel mixture with no changes to the timing, the horsepower is up to 91.66 and torque goes up to 103.53 ft. lbs. That's a gain of 22.01 hp and 14.63 ft. lbs. of torque, quite an improvement.

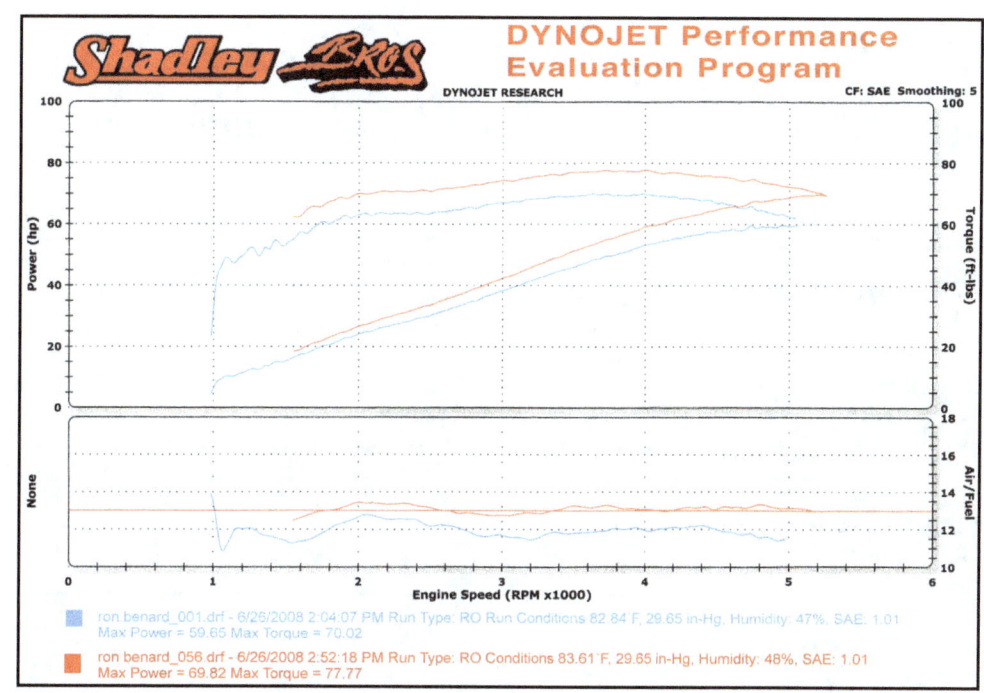

The blue lines indicate the before condition, and the red is the final, improved results. The air-fuel graph is at the very bottom. An ideal air-fuel line runs horizontally across the graph like the red "after" line does here.

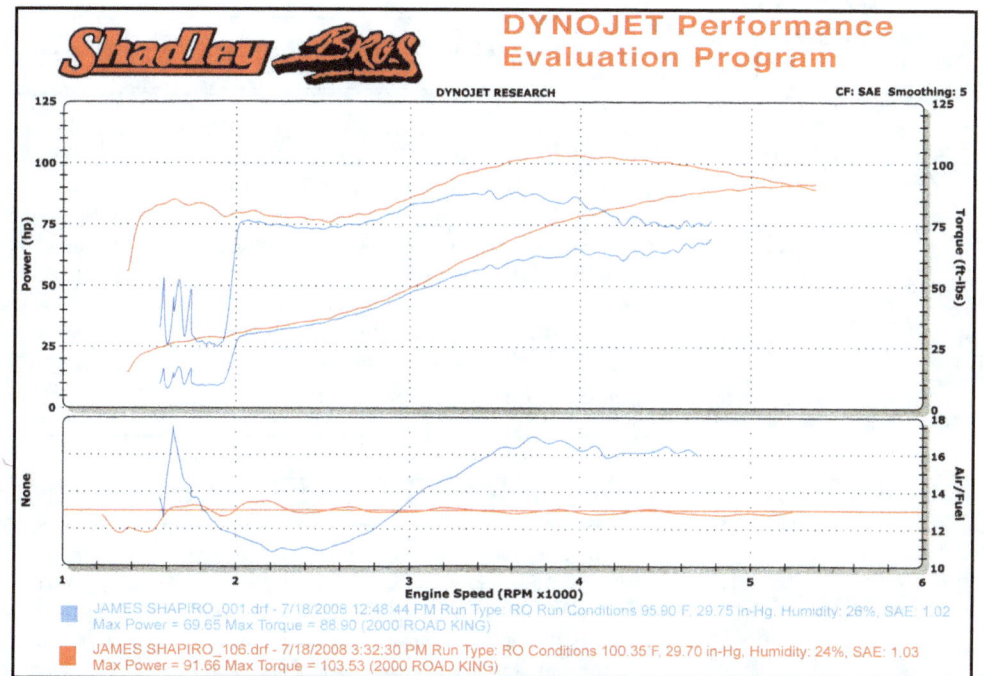

To say that the air-fuel line is way off on the before graph is an understatement. Note the correlation between the the shape of the original air-fuel line and the horsepower and torque graphs at the same RPM.

Wolfgang Books On The Web
http://www.wolfpub.com

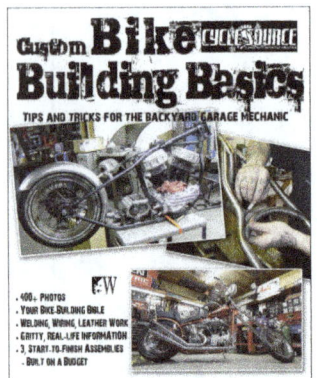

CUSTOM BIKE BUILDING BASICS

Custom Bike Building Basics is the basic bible that at-home builders need to build and modify their own motorcycle.

But first you need a place to work and a set of tools to work with. Chapter One covers these topics and more, including the need for a quality compressor and a decent motorcycle lift. Basic skill building is next, starting with Steel Fabrication and Welding.

Grass roots bikes are often built using a "donor bike" as the foundation and source for the majority of parts. Chapters Four and Five offer tips on choosing the best donor bike.

The final topics are two that we often find intimidating: Upholstery and Wiring. With one chapter on each Topic, the mystery and fear are eliminated.

Sixteen Chapters   144 Pages $24.95   Over 450 photos, 100% color

TATTOO BIBLE BOOK THREE

Book Three, the newest installment in the popular Superior Tattoo Bible series, continues the tradition of offering a vast collection of only the best tattoo artwork available.

Unlike the earlier Bibles, Tattoo Bible Book Three is a collection of designs from opposite ends of the spectrum. This new book contains images from both the old school and the new. Among this expanse of flash are colorful images of sacred hearts, and black and grey representations of Celtic knots.

Book Three showcases artwork from some of the most-recognizable names in the tattoo world, as well as the coolest, trendiest designs from some of the newest, up-and-coming talent in the industry!

Nine Chapters   144 Pages $27.95   Over 350 photos

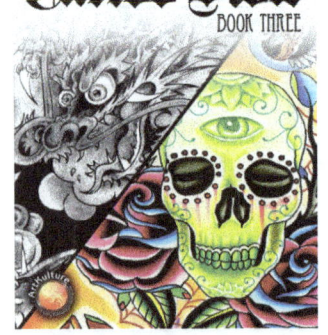

HOW-TO BUILD A CHEAP CHOPPER

Choppers don't have to cost $30,000. In fact, a chopper built from the right parts can be assembled for as little as $5,000. How to Build a Cheap Chopper documents the construction of 4 choppers with complete start-to-finish sequences photographed in the shops of Tom Summers, Donnie Smith, Brian Klock and Dave Perewitz.

Least expensive is the metric chopper, based on a Japanese 4-cylinder engine and transmission installed in a hardtail frame. Next up, price wise, are 2 bikes built using Buell/Sportster drivetrains. The recipe here is simple; combine one used Buell or Sportster with a hardtail frame for an almost instant chopper. The big twin chopper is the least cheap of the 4, yet it's still far less expensive than most bikes built today. Cheap Chopper uses 144 pages and over 400 color images to completely explain each assembly.

Eleven Chapters   144 Pages $27.95   Over 400 photos, 100% color

KOSMOSKI'S NEW KUSTOM PAINTING SECRETS

Jon Kosmoski - the King of Kustom Painters - puts over four decades of experience into Kosmoski's New Kustom Painting Secrets. Jon starts with the basics: how to set up a shop, pick a compressor, and prepare the metal. Next comes a thorough discussion of modern paint: What it is, how it's made and which type is best suited to custom paintwork.

How to pick, adjust and use spray guns makes up the next section in Jon's new book. As Jon explains, "you need to have the gun adjusted properly, and the way to do that is with test panels done before you start the paint job." The test panels included in the book show a good and bad pattern, and how to adjust a gun that's putting out a flawed pattern.

Eight Chapters   144 Pages $27.95   Over 400 photos, 100% color

More Great Books From Wolfgang Publications!
http://www.wolfpub.com

ILLUSTRATED HISTORY
Ultimate Triumph Collection	$49.95

BIKER BASICS
Custom Bike Building Basics	$24.95
Custom Bike Building ADVANCED	$24.95
Sportster/Buell Engine Hop-Up Guide	$24.95
Sheet Metal Fabrication Basics	$24.95

COMPOSITE GARAGE
Composite Materials Handbook #1	$27.95
Composite Materials Handbook #2	$27.95
Composite Materials Handbook #3	$27.95

HOT ROD BASICS
Hot Rod Wiring	$27.95
How to Chop Tops	$24.95
How to Air Condition Your Hot Rod	$24.95

MOTORCYCLE RESTORATION SERIES
Triumph Restoration - Unit 650cc	$29.95
Triumph MC Restoration Pre-Unit	$29.95

CUSTOM BUILDER SERIES
How to Build A Café Racer	$27.95
Advanced Custom Motorcycle Wiring - Revised	$27.95
How to Build an Old Skool Bobber Sec Ed	$27.95
How To Build The Ultimate V-Twin Motorcycle	$24.95
Advanced Custom Motorcycle Assembly & Fabrication	$27.95
Advanced Custom Motorcycle Chassis	$27.95
How to Build a Cheap Chopper	$27.95
How to Build a Chopper	$27.95

SHEET METAL
Advanced Sheet Metal Fabrication	$27.95
Ultimate Sheet Metal Fabrication	$24.95
Sheet Metal Bible	$29.95

AIR SKOOL SKILLS
Airbrush Bible	$29.95
How Airbrushes Work	$24.95

PAINT EXPERT
How To Airbrush, Pinstripe & Goldleaf	$27.95
Kosmoski's New Kustom Painting Secrets	$27.95
Advanced Custom Motorcycle Painting	$27.95
Pro Pinstripe Techniques	$27.95
Advanced Pinstripe Art	$27.95

TATTOO U Series
Into The Skin The Ultimate Tattoo Sourcebook	$34.95
Tattoo Sketch Book	$32.95
American Tattoos	$27.95
Tattoo - From Idea to Ink	$27.95
Advanced Tattoo Art	$27.95
Tattoo Bible Book One	$27.95
Tattoo Bible Book Two	$27.95
Tattoo Bible Book Three	$27.95

NOTEWORTHY
American Police Motorcycles - Revised	$24.95
Guitar Building Basics Acoustic Assembly at Home	$27.95

LIFESTYLE
Bean're — Motorcycle Nomad	$18.95
The Colorful World of Tattoo Models	$34.95

Shadley Bros.
115 Bedford St.
PO Box 127
Whitman, MA 02382
781 447 4454
Web: www.shadleybros.com